Celebr
Our Faith

Confirmation

Our Father
H M
G B
A C
A C

Margaret Hanrahan, D. Min.

write letter
why? & wont to be con.

MSGR. David Slubercky
1 page

♣ BROWN-ROA
A Division of Harcourt Brace & Company

5 8th No class our of your
following week Test

Nihil Obstat

Rev. Richard L. Schaefer

Imprimatur

✠ Most Rev. Jerome Hanus, OSB
Archbishop of Dubuque
January 25, 1999
Feast of the Conversion of Saint Paul

The Ad Hoc Committee to Oversee the Use of the Catechism, National Conference of Catholic Bishops, has found this catechetical program, copyright 2000, to be in conformity with the *Catechism of the Catholic Church*.

The nihil obstat and imprimatur are official declarations that a book or pamphlet is free of doctrinal or moral error. No implication is contained herein that those who granted the nihil obstat and imprimatur agree with the contents, opinions, or statements expressed.

BROWN-ROA

A Division of Harcourt Brace & Company

Our Mission

The primary mission of BROWN-ROA is to provide the Catholic markets with the highest quality catechetical print and media resources. The content of these resources reflects the best insights of current theology, methodology, and pedagogical research. These resources are practical and easy to use, designed to meet expressed market needs, and written to reflect the teachings of the Catholic Church.

Printed in the United States of America

ISBN 0-15-950573-9

10   9

Celebrating Our Faith

Confirmation

My Confirmation

I will celebrate the Sacrament of Confirmation

on

_____

date

at

_____

name of church

My Confirmation name is

_____

My sponsor/mentor is

_____

The presider will be

_____

_____

pastor's name

_____

catechist's name

A Mentor and Candidate Prayer

"You have been trusted with a wonderful treasure. Guard it with the help of the Holy Spirit, who lives within you."

—2 Timothy 1:14

Together: God the Father, we thank you for the faith we have in common. Jesus, Son of God, we praise you for coming to earth to show us how to live. Holy Spirit, guide our time together.

Now we have received not the spirit of the world, but the Spirit that is from God, so that we may understand the gifts bestowed on us by God. And we speak of these things in words not taught by human wisdom but taught by the Spirit, interpreting spiritual things to those who are spiritual.

—1 Corinthians 2:12–13

Mentor: Spirit of God, be with me as I spend time with this candidate preparing for the Sacrament of Confirmation. Give me the gift of understanding so I will be able to listen patiently. Bestow on me wisdom and knowledge to share my faith.

Candidate: Spirit of God, be with me as I spend time with my mentor. Give me the gift of courage to live my faith openly. Open my mind and heart to the counsel given me by my mentor.

Together: During our time together may we develop a deeper reverence and awe of God.

*Come, Holy Spirit, fill the hearts of your faithful,
And kindle in them the fire of your love.
Send forth your Spirit and they shall be created.
And you will renew the face of the earth. Amen.*

NAMED AND CALLED

Map of the Journey

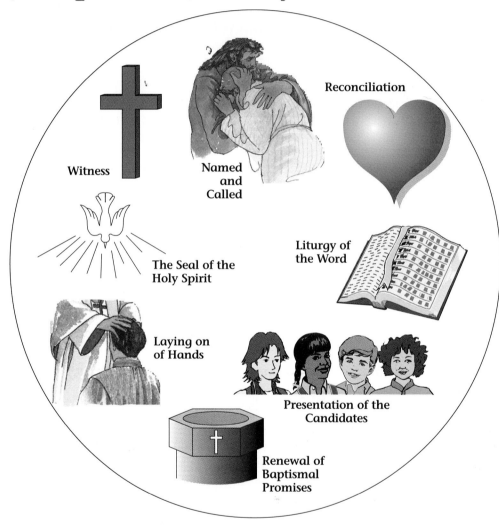

Witness

Named and Called

Reconciliation

The Seal of the Holy Spirit

Liturgy of the Word

Laying on of Hands

Presentation of the Candidates

Renewal of Baptismal Promises

But now thus says the Lord, he who created you, O Jacob,
he who formed you, O Israel:
Do not fear, for I have redeemed you;
I have called you by name, you are mine
—Isaiah 43:1

Guides Along the Way

Role of the adult family member

1. Models the commitment to personal prayer, community worship, and ministry expected of a mature Christian.

2. Assumes responsibility to assist the candidate in meeting the program's attendance and service requirements.

3. Agrees to help the candidate process the experience of the journey—enters into dialogue with the candidate, prays for and with the candidate, is willing to share his or her personal faith story with the candidate.

4. Is willing to step in for the mentor at any time if the mentor is unable to fulfill his or her commitment.

Role of the sponsor/mentor

1. Models the commitment to personal prayer, community worship, and ministry expected of a mature Christian.

2. Agrees to attend the sessions with the candidate.

3. Willingly shares his or her faith story with the candidate in both formal and informal settings.

4. Supports the candidate during the journey of preparation through ongoing dialogue, notes of encouragement, and a willingness to listen to the concerns and hopes of the candidate.

5. Prays for and with the candidate.

6. If the mentor is going to be the candidate's sponsor, this person must be a confirmed, practicing Catholic, sufficiently mature for this role, and not prohibited by law for serving in this capacity. The sponsor presents the candidate to the bishop or other appointed minister for the anointing and with the help of the Holy Spirit will continue to guide the newly confirmed in the future.

No Parents

Catholic Beliefs

Sacraments of Initiation

Baptism, Confirmation, and Eucharist are the Sacraments of Initiation. Although Confirmation is sometimes called the "sacrament of Christian maturity" (*Catechism of the Catholic Church*, 1308), this can be misleading. For many young people "becoming an adult in the Church" might mean they have completed learning about their faith. In reality, Confirmation should deepen our understanding of and participation in our Catholic faith and community. Confirmation completes and seals our Baptism. Through the fullness of the Spirit's gifts, we are led to Eucharist through which we become the Body of Christ.

Quest of Intellect and Heart

Preparing for the reception of the sacrament is far more than an intellectual quest, though you are asked to attend Confirmation classes. The whole person—mind, body, heart, and spirit—must be addressed. Therefore, Confirmation preparation is much like going on a journey. The process should be seen as part of your larger faith journey. You, by virtue of your Baptism, have been initiated into the pilgrim people of God. To be prepared you must study, reflect on your life, pray, and do service. You will need support during this period of preparation. Talking with your family members, with a sponsor or mentor, with the catechist, and with other candidates is important.

Parish Community Role

The role of your local parish community is also important. What, after all, are you being initiated into but a deeper union with God and the Church. Use of the parish worship space is used in this session. Moving into the worship space is meant to communicate not only a sense of the sacred but a sense of belonging to your parish faith community, who gathers in this space to praise and worship God and join in communion with one another. It is important that you understand as you begin the Confirmation process that you are welcomed and supported—named and called—to continue your journey toward full communion with the Catholic Church.

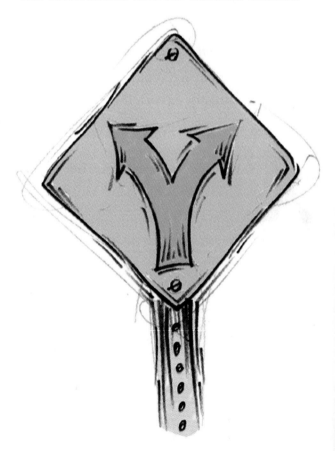

Candidate and Family Roles

You and your families are being challenged to take the Confirmation process seriously. The expectations of all involved are clearly stated in this session. This is not a class; this is a journey. This journey demands time, energy, commitment, and dedication by all involved. Are you and your support community ready?

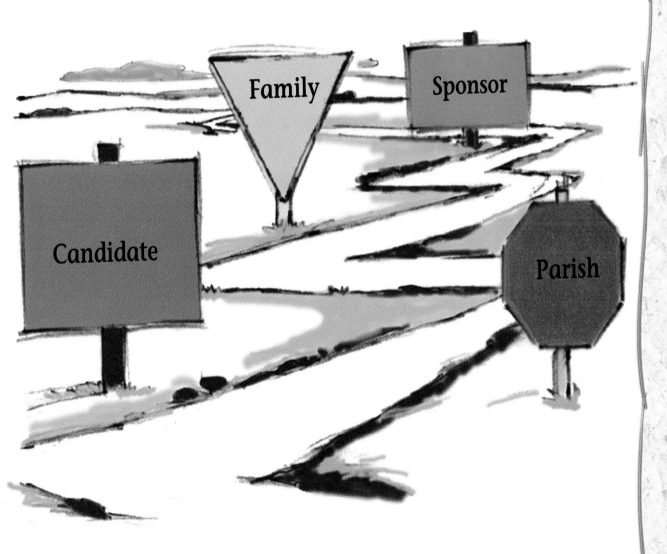

Expectations of the Candidates

1. Enter the journey with a willing heart and an open mind.
2. Commit oneself to consistent personal prayer throughout the journey.
3. Attend all sessions.
4. Willingly engage in community service.
5. Participate in the Confirmation retreat.
6. Complete all entries in the candidate's book.
7. Support and encourage other candidates on the journey.
8. Maintain an open and honest relationship with one's sponsor or mentor.

Confirmation Covenant

I _____, with the support of
my family and my mentor, _____,
commit myself to complete my sacramental initiation by preparing to
receive the Sacrament of Confirmation. I fully understand that by
committing myself to this process, I accept the responsibility to learn
more about my faith, to serve others willingly, to reflect on my
relationship with the Holy Spirit, and to become a witness to the gospel
values and moral precepts of the Church.

_____   _____
Candidate's Signature   Date

_____   _____
Witness's Signature   Date

Discernment Questions

This page is designed so the book can be placed between the family member and the candidate and both can answer questions at the same time.

Questions for the candidate.

How do my actions and my personal prayer indicate at this time that I want to actively practice my faith?

I read the Bible every day, try to understand it, pray several times a day

How open am I to listening to the wisdom offered to me by others about my faith?

How important to me is regular attendance at Mass?

I attend mass regularly w/ my family I find it to be very important

What actions am I willing to take to show my commitment and dedication to the Confirmation process?

Questions for the family member.

How can I, through my actions and my prayer, help ready this candidate for Confirmation?

How comfortable am I listening to, talking with, and praying with this candidate about my faith?

How does my life model the importance of regular Mass attendance?

How will I prioritize my other commitments to encourage the candidate's commitment to this process?

An Adventurer on a Journey

Journey has been our theme for this session. Perhaps no saint could be a better example for someone setting out on a faith journey than the Celtic Saint Brendan of Clonfert.

Brendan was born in the year A.D. 486 on the west coast of Ireland. Before Brendan was born, as the story goes, his mother had a dream. When she told her dream to the bishop, he said she would give birth to a extraordinary child who would be filled with the grace of the Holy Spirit. Mobi was the name Brendan's parents first gave to him, but he was so fair of body and soul that they changed his name to Brendan, which means "fair drop."

As a young man Brendan was known for his spirit of adventure and his willingness to take risks. He studied the Scriptures and became a monk. Brendan felt God was calling him to some great unknown adventure. He spoke to many people and thought hard about what he should do with his life. Finally, Brendan met a holy man named Barinthus, who told him of a mysterious island that he and his son had discovered called the Land of Saints.

Hearing this story, Brendan knew that God was calling him to journey to the Land of Saints.

Brendan spent his life with his companions, searching out the Land of Saints. We don't know if he ever found it, but we do know that he discovered many other islands. He brought the story of Christ to all those who lived in these places. His willingness to go where God led him, braving the hardships and danger of travel at sea—storms, hunger, and loneliness—while remaining faithful to God's plan for him, made Brendan a holy man.

—Sellner, Edward C. Adapted from *Wisdom of Celtic Saints*. Notre Dame: Ave Maria Press, 1993.

You have been called to a great adventure, a wondrous journey. God is calling you. What risks are you taking by beginning this journey?

Who can help you follow Brendan's example and support you as you meet each new challenge?
Family and Friend's can help.

Only you can decide. As you make your decision, however, pray to Saint Brendan. He knows all about the fear and the risks of pioneering a new journey. He also knows all the joys and great excitement of journeying with the Lord.

Scripture

. . . I pledged myself to you and entered into a covenant with you, says the Lord God, and you became mine (Ezekiel 16:8).

Now the boy Samuel was ministering to the Lord under Eli. The word of the Lord was rare in those days; visions were not widespread.

At that time Eli, whose eyesight had begun to grow dim so that he could not see, was lying down in his room; the lamp of God had not yet gone out, and Samuel was lying down in the temple of the Lord, where the ark of God was. Then the Lord called, "Samuel! Samuel!" and he said, "Here I am!" and ran to Eli, and said, "Here I am, for you called me." But he said, "I did not call; lie down again." So he went and lay down. The Lord called again, "Samuel!" Samuel got up and went to Eli, and said, "Here I am, for you called me." But he said, "I did not call, my son; lie down again." Now Samuel did not yet know the Lord, and the word of the Lord had not yet been revealed to him. The Lord called Samuel again, a third time. And he got up and went to Eli, and said, "Here I am, for you called me." Then Eli perceived that the Lord was calling the boy. Therefore Eli said to Samuel, "Go, lie down; and if he calls you, you shall say, 'Speak, Lord, for your servant is listening" (1 Samuel 3:1–9).

Language of Faith

Call In the biblical sense, to be called means to be chosen. In Baptism we are chosen by God to share more fully in the mystery of divine life and love and to be welcomed into the Church. In Confirmation we are called to deepen our relationship with God by becoming more aware of God's presence in our life. We answer to the call by participating more fully in the mission and ministry of the Church.

Covenant A sacred promise or agreement made between two parties. All Christian covenants are modeled on the relationship between God and his people. God made a covenant with Israel and renewed it often. Jesus' sacrifice established the new and everlasting covenant, open to all who do God's will. In this session you are asked to make a solemn promise between you, God, and the faith community. You promise to undertake the preparation for Confirmation, the faith community promises to support you, and God promises to be with you.

Confirmation name The name of a saint is chosen by the person being confirmed to signify his or her identity as a disciple of Christ. According to diocesan guidelines, the confirmand can choose his or her baptismal name, or an additional name can be added to his or her baptismal name.

Sacraments of Initiation Baptism, Eucharist, and Confirmation are called the *Sacraments of Initiation*. These sacraments make us children of God and full members of Christ's Church.

3. fulfillment?

RECONCILIATION

Discernment Questions

This page is designed so the book can be placed between the mentor and the candidate and both can answer questions at the same time.

I am excited about this step of my faith journey because . . . *It will bring me closer to God*

A reason why I have chosen you for my mentor is . . .

One reason why I have chosen to continue in the Confirmation process is . . . *God is an important part of my life*

Questions for the candidate.

Questions for the mentor.

How do my actions and my personal prayer life indicate to me at this time that I would be a good role model for this candidate?

What is one reason why I think this candidate may have chosen me to be his or her mentor?

What other commitments may I have to reprioritize to be able to have time to listen, talk, and pray with this candidate?

The Fall

Before the Fall, how does the author describe the relationships in the garden
• between Adam and Eve?

• between humans and God?

• between the people and nature?

What attitude do you think led to the first sin?

As a result of the first sin, what changed
• between Adam and Eve?

• between humans and God?

• between the people and nature?

Parish Reconciliation Opportunities

An examination of conscience and the Rite for Individual and Communal reception of the Sacrament of Reconciliation can be found on pages 81 and 82.

Date:

Time:

Catholic Beliefs

Reality of Sin

All of us are affected by the reality of sin. Once suspicion, dishonesty, anger, and jealousy entered the world, there was no turning back. The presence of sin cannot be denied because no one escapes the experience of evil and suffering (*Catechism of the Catholic Church*, 385, 386).

We are all sinners. We all, at some time and in some way, oppose God's plan for the world. We think and act in ways that hurt ourselves as well as others. The *Catechism of the Catholic Church* states: "To try to understand what sin is, one must first recognize the profound relationship of man to God, for only in this relationship is the evil of sin unmasked in its true identity as humanity's rejection of God and opposition to him. . ." (386).

Consequences of Sin

It is easy for us to see the marked difference sin makes. Prior to sin, everything existed in its created state of original holiness and original goodness. Harmony and trust were normal. Love was generously shared, and there was no experience of pain or death. After sin, nothing was the same. The final and most profound consequence of sin is death (CCC, 400). At this age death may seem a long time away, however you do experience small deaths—divorce, illness, disappointment, failure, the end of relationships, and so on.

Effects of Sin

The most common effect of sin that the majority of us experience is its impact on relationships. It is clear from the story in Genesis that sin radically changes relationships. Before the fall, the relationship between Adam, Eve, and God was one of openness, trust, friendship, caring, unity, love, respect, and joy. The relationship between people and nature was one of harmony, peace, abundance, delight, and so on. But sin changed all that. After the loss of original justice, relationships were fractured by mistrust, dishonesty, violence, pain, greed, pride, selfishness, anger, sadness, loneliness, and jealousy. As a result of original sin, humans became subject to ignorance, suffering, temptation, and inclined to sin (CCC, 418).

Social Dimensions of Sin

We readily understand the impact sin has on us as individuals. We know what it feels like to be ignored, excluded, lied to, abused physically and emotionally. We feel the pain when we are sinned against and the guilt when we sin against another. But sin also affects society (CCC, 408). Think about how you feel when two of your friends are fighting. Doesn't their anger affect you even if you are not directly involved in the fight? Think about how people's carelessness and disrespect affect the environment—yours as well as theirs. Sin is like throwing a stone into a pond. There is the initial effect, but then the effect ripples.

Repairing Sin

Jesus is the Word through whom the world was created (John 1:1). The world is a reflection of his being and his relationship with his Father. God the Father sent his Son into the world to repair what sin had destroyed. Through the saving action of Jesus' sacrifice on the cross, God and the world were reconciled in a way we could not do for ourselves. Jesus proclaimed the kingdom of God. As disciples of Christ our Savior, we follow the will of God and act in union with him. In and through Christ we build the kingdom of God on earth (CCC, 421, 479). We as disciples of Christ have to actively repair the damage that has been done by sin. The followers of Jesus must reject the ways of evil and work for peace and justice. Jesus proclaimed the reign of God. Through the celebration of the Sacrament of Confirmation, we embrace God's reign as our own. Saint Paul calls this "putting on the mind of Christ." Saved by Jesus we are called to incorporate his teachings and examples in our lives. We have

to replace dishonesty with honesty, sadness with joy, violence with peace, selfishness with compassion, despair with hope, brokenness with forgiveness. This is the reconciling ministry of Jesus which we as Church continue in his name and by his power.

Continuing Jesus' Work

Through the Sacrament of Reconciliation the Church continues, in the power of the Holy Spirit, Jesus' work of healing and salvation (CCC, 1421). As disciples of Jesus we need to acknowledge our own sinfulness and ask for forgiveness. We also need to do whatever is in our power to repair the damage sin has caused. Through his teachings Jesus invites us to be part of the kingdom. Within the kingdom of God, words are not enough; action is also required. As disciples of Jesus, we act in union with him to build up the kingdom of God on earth. Later in the Confirmation preparation process, you will be asked to do community service. Start thinking about what you can do, how you can use your gifts and talents to make the world a better place.

The Holy Spirit

We must be open to and rely on the guidance and strength of the Holy Spirit (CCC, 1285) and accept and use the gifts offered by the Holy Spirit through the Sacrament of Confirmation. The Holy Spirit through the teaching Church guides our decisions, inspires us to do what is right. We need to trust the Spirit and ask for guidance and strength to follow the Ten commandments and live the Beatitudes (CCC, 1303).

God's Plan for Loving Relationships

The Ten Commandments are engraved by God in the human heart. They tell us what love of God and love of neighbor require. We come to understand God's revelation of the Commandments through the teaching Church and our conscience.

The Ten Commandments

1. **I am the Lord your God. You shall not have strange gods before me.**

   Put God first in your life before all things.

2. **You shall not take the name of the Lord your God in vain.**

   Respect God's name and holy things. Don't curse or use bad language.

3. **Remember to keep holy the Lord's day.**

   Take part in the Mass on Sundays and holy days. Avoid unnecessary work on these days.

4. **Honor your father and your mother.**

   Obey and show respect to parents and other people in proper authority.

5. **You shall not kill.**

   Respect and protect life—our own and that of others.

6. **You shall not commit adultery.**

   Show respect for marriage and family life. Respect God's gift of sexuality.

7. **You shall not steal.**

   Respect the things that belong to others. Share what you have with those in need. Work for justice.

8. **You shall not bear false witness against your neighbor.**

   Be honest and truthful. Don't make fun of others.

9. **You shall not covet your neighbor's wife.**

   Be faithful to family members and friends. Don't be jealous.

10. **You shall not covet your neighbor's goods.**

    Rejoice in others' good fortune. Don't envy what other people have. Don't be greedy.

Jesus' Path to the Kingdom

The Beatitudes are at the heart of Jesus' preaching. They help us discern the actions and attitudes necessary to live a Christian life.

The Beatitudes

God blesses those people who depend only on him.
   They belong to the kingdom of heaven!

   Don't let material things get in the way of loving God and others.

God blesses those people who grieve.
   They will find comfort!

   Share other people's sorrows and joys.

God blesses those people who are humble.
   The earth will belong to them!

   Learn to be gentle with people and things.

God blesses those people who want to obey him more than to eat or drink.
   They will be given what they want!

   Work hard to make sure that all people are treated justly.

God blesses those people who are merciful.
   They will be treated with mercy!

   Forgive others and ask their forgiveness.

God blesses those people whose hearts are pure.
   They will see him!

   Turn your attention only toward what is good and right.

God blesses those people who make peace.
   They will be called his children!

   Look for ways to solve problems peacefully.

God blesses those people who are treated badly for doing right.
   They belong to the kingdom of heaven!

   In difficult times, keep trusting in God and standing up for what is right.

Matthew 5:3–10, The HOLY BIBLE: Contemporary English Version, © American Bible Society, 1991.

Dream about what the world would be like if we all lived as disciples of Jesus. How would the Ten Commandments, Beatitudes, and the guidance of the teaching Church help?

Sinner Becomes Saint

Augustine of Hippo was born in A.D. 354 in North Africa. Augustine was raised as a Christian but rebelled early in his life. A brilliant young student, he was an avid reader and loved to learn. Augustine wanted more out of life than the safe, comfortable, and somewhat boring existence of his parents. As a teenager he made his way to the city of Carthage, the capital of Roman Africa.

Here the young Augustine saw and experienced all kinds of new things. Pursuing his love of learning, he continued to read and seek out the best teachers. He also experimented with alcohol, sex, and gambling. But none of these activities filled the emptiness inside this restless young man.

Augustine eventually took a teaching position at Carthage. But his mind and soul were still restless. There must be more, he thought. In Milan, he went to hear Bishop Ambrose preach. Ambrose was a dynamic preacher, and for the first time, Augustine began to see how Christianity could help him make sense of his world and answer his questions. He studied earnestly under Saint Ambrose, and at the age of thirty-two, Augustine was baptized.

Augustine returned to his native Africa and was ordained a priest and later a bishop. He wrote several books and preached to all who would listen. Many of our teachings and Church practices come to us from Augustine. In addition to his great intellect, he was known as a kind and charitable person, devoted to his people. Augustine lived a very simple life in common with his priests and did much to foster the creation of religious communities. One such community of priests, the Augustinians, is named after him.

—Coulson, John, ed. *The Saints A Concise Biographical Dictionary.* New York: Hawthorn Books, 1958.

—Cahill, Thomas. *How the Irish Saved Civilization.* Doubleday: New York, 1996.

Saint Augustine spoke of his own sinfulness often. He is a powerful model of how people can change. Though a great sinner, Augustine knew that there is no sin God will not forgive if the penitent is truly sorry. He responded to the Gospel call to repent and he reformed his life. In doing so Augustine became one of the great scholars and saints of our tradition.

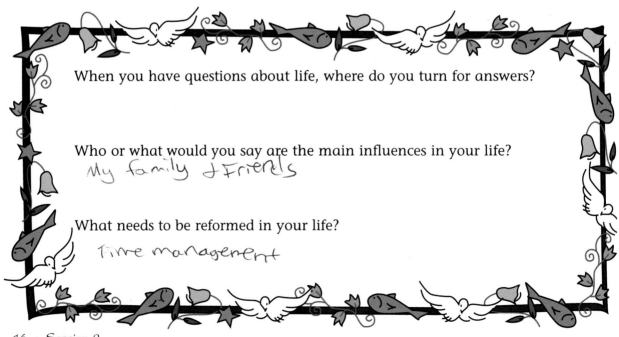

When you have questions about life, where do you turn for answers?

Who or what would you say are the main influences in your life?

My family & Friends

What needs to be reformed in your life?

Time management

Scripture

Therefore confess your sins to one another, and pray for one another so that you may be healed (James 5:16).

And during supper Jesus, knowing that the Father had given all things into his hands, and that he had come from God and was going to God, got up from the table, took off his outer robe, and tied a towel around himself. Then he poured water into a basin and began to wash the disciples' feet and to wipe them with the towel that was tied around him. . . . After he had washed their feet, had put on his robe, and had returned to the table, he said to them, "Do you know what I have done to you? You call me Teacher and Lord—and you are right, for that is what I am. So if I, your Lord and Teacher, have washed your feet, you also ought to wash one another's feet. For I have set you an example, that you also should do as I have done to you (John 13:2b–5; 12–15).

Language of Faith

Sin   Sin is an unloving choice and the unloving actions that come from that choice. You sin when you turn away from God, other people, or yourself. Sin can be serious (mortal) or less serious (venial). In order for sin to be mortal, it must be a serious matter. You must know that it is seriously wrong. And you must choose it anyway. Venial sin is less serious than mortal sin. Venial sin comes from laziness and bad habits. It weakens your relationship with God and others. Every sin, no matter how serious, can be forgiven if you are truly sorry.

Reconciliation   A process whereby you reestablish or rebuild a relationship damaged by sin. The first step in this process is your recognition and acknowledgment that you have done wrong. You must then be sorry for the wrong you have done and be willing to change your attitude and behavior. As a disciple of Jesus, you should ask for, and give others, the gift of forgiveness. The Church celebrates this reality in the Sacrament of Reconciliation, or Penance.

Purification   To be purified is to be made clean. The most important purification rite for Christians is Baptism—you were washed in the waters of Baptism and asked to reject evil and declare your belief in God.

The Ten Commandments   These laws of God help us show love for God and others.

Beatitudes These sayings of Jesus summarize the way to live in God's kingdom and point the way to true happiness.

Teaching Church   With the guidance of the Holy Spirit, the bishops in union with the pope along with the priests have the duty to preach the gospel and to preserve the truth of the faith for the Church. This teaching office of the Church is called the magisterium.

SCRIPTURE AND THE HOLY SPIRIT

Bible IQ

Together with your mentor, read each statement and on the line write whether you think the statement is *true* or *false*.

_____ 1. The Bible is divided into four major parts.

_____ 2. There are more than 55 books in the Old Testament.

_____ 3. The gospels are located in the New Testament in the Bible.

_____ 4. The Bible contains letters from the apostles to their friends.

_____ 5. The Old Testament doesn't apply to today's world.

_____ 6. God is the author of Scripture.

_____ 7. The Bible is a strict eyewitness account of historical facts.

_____ 8. Sometimes our understanding of a particular passage of the Bible changes.

_____ 9. The guidance of the Holy Spirit is necessary to correctly understand the Bible.

_____ 10. Books are still being added to the Bible.

The Bible—An Ancient Library

The Bible is one book made up of many books. Using a Bible for reference, write in the names of the Old Testament and New Testament books.

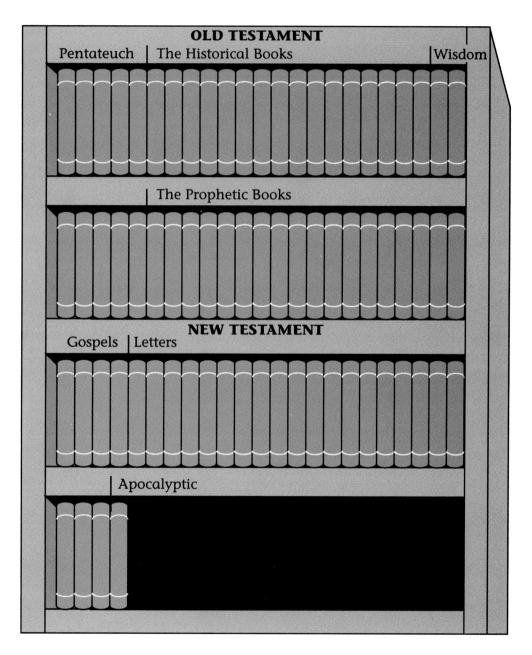

The books of the Bible were written over thousands of years by many different authors. These authors wrote in many different kinds of literary styles. There are law books, histories, myths, census records, letters, biographies, prayers, song lyrics, and poetry. As Catholics we believe that the Holy Spirit inspired the writers of the biblical books. That is why we say that the Bible is the word of God.

Catholic Beliefs

A Library of Writings

It might be more accurate to think of the Bible as a library of books rather than a single book. The Catholic canon of Scripture contains two testaments—the Old Testament, comprised of 46 books, and the New Testament, which contains 27 books. The Gospels, found in the New Testament, play a central role in Scripture for Christians. They are the primary source for the life and teachings of Jesus Christ, who is the living word of God.

A Library of Styles

In addition to containing a number of books, the Bible uses many literary forms. For example, Genesis is a collection of sagas or epic narratives about the beginnings of creation and the origins of the Hebrew people. The Book of Deuteronomy could be referred to as a law book; 1 and 2 Kings could be classified as history books. The truth which God put into Scripture cannot be fully understood by looking at individual passages or individual books. Therefore, each book should be seen in relation to all the other books. The complete truth can be known only through the whole.

Oral Tradition

The Bible was actually composed in two stages. The first was the oral stage. Stories of God's dealings with his people were kept alive through their telling and retelling. The older generation memorized them and taught them to the next generation, who in turn passed them on to the future generations. Various people remembered different parts of the same story, so stories about the same event sometimes sounded very different.

Written Through the Inspiration of the Spirit

God authored Scripture by inspiring certain people to be human authors and use their talents as writers, prophets, and teachers to record the oral stories. God inspired these people through the Holy Spirit to reveal himself and open up the possibility of a conversation between God and humans. "Sacred Scripture is the speech of God as it is put down in writing under the breath of the Holy Spirit" [DV 9] (CCC, 81). That same Spirit inspired and enlightened the apostles and their successors "that they may faithfully preserve, expound, and spread [the word of God] abroad by their preaching" [DV 9] (CCC, 81). Furthermore the Church teaches that the Holy Spirit continues to be an active agent in this revelatory process. Study and prayer are necessary so that your mind and heart will be open to the word of God in order that you may understand more clearly what God is saying.

Literal Versus Contextual

Scripture is interpreted in a contextual, or spiritual, sense and not just a literal sense. Fundamentalist Christians believe that what is written in the Bible is mostly fact. This is a literal interpretation of Scripture. Catholics and many other Christians interpret the Bible in a contextual, or spiritual, sense (CCC, 115–117). This means that you look into the meaning or deeper truths behind and through the actual words. The Bible is a religious book, a statement of theologies, a summary of beliefs, not simply a strict eyewitness account of historical facts.

Tic-Tac-Toe Word Game

Directions: To win a person must have three Xs or Os in a vertical, horizontal, or diagonal line. To place a mark in a square, look at the word or phrase at the top of the column and the beginning of the row. You must use both words or phrases constructively in a sentence in order to mark that square on the grid. To place a mark in square 1, you must use the words *sin* and *call* in a sentence. To place a mark in square 5, you must use the words *New Testament* and *Beatitudes* in a sentence. To place a mark in square 9, you must use *divine inspiration* and *reconciliation* in a sentence. Once you have three marks in a row, you have completed the exercise.

	Call	New Testament	Reconciliation
Sin	1	2	3
Beatitudes	4	5	6
Divine Inspiration	7	8	9

Write your sentences in the space below.

_____

_____

_____

_____

_____

_____

_____

_____

_____

My Understanding of the Bible

Questions for the candidate.

Based on the information given in this session, what do I now understand about the Bible that I didn't understand before?

About what in the Bible am I still confused?

Think of a Bible story that relates to the Sacrament of Confirmation. What new insights do I have about this story now that I am going through the Confirmation process?

Questions for the mentor.

Based on the information given in this session, what do I now understand about the Bible that I didn't understand before?

About what in the Bible am I still confused?

Think of a Bible story that relates to the Sacrament of Confirmation. What new insights do I have about this story now that I am a mentor in the Confirmation process?

An Inspired Writer

All of Scripture is divinely inspired, meaning that the Holy Spirit worked through human authors. One of these writers was Mark the Evangelist. His house was used as the house where people gathered to listen to the teachings of the apostles. Saint Peter was a frequent guest and may even have lived with Mark for a time. At the end of his life, Peter referred to Mark as *"my son Mark"* (1 Peter 5:13). Much of what Mark later chose to write in his Gospel may have come from the stories Peter shared with him.

Not only was Mark at the center of the activity in the Christian community in Jerusalem, but we know from the Acts of the Apostles that he accompanied Barnabas, Mark's cousin, and Paul on their first missionary journey. No doubt some of what Mark learned from Paul also found its way into his Gospel.

Mark must have spent considerable time in Rome, as it was to the Roman Christians that Mark wrote his Gospel. The Christians in Rome were suffering great hardships, and many were being put to death, perhaps including Mark's mentors, Peter and Paul. The Roman Christians were frightened and often discouraged. Mark, calling on the stories he heard as a young person in his home and the lessons he learned along the way with Barnabas, wrote a message of hope. Through the guidance of the Holy Spirit, Mark proclaimed that God understood what the Christians were going through. He encouraged them to remember that Jesus suffered and died for them.

Mark's spiritual journey, not unlike our own, began when he was young, in the house in which he was raised. He had the good fortune to meet some powerful and faith-filled people in those early days and to participate in some significant events. He remembered what he was taught and the stories he heard, and most importantly, he shared them with others.

—Attwater, Donald. *The Avenel Dictionary of Saints.* New York: Avenel Books, 1981.

—Farmer, David Hugh, ed. *Butler's Lives of the Saints.* Collegeville, MN: The Liturgical Press, 1996.

—Coulson, John, ed. *The Saints: A Concise Biographical Dictionary.* New York: Hawthorn Books, Inc., 1958.

Mark was not the best writer. Scripture scholars tell us Mark's Gospel is filled with grammatical problems, but it is faith-filled and sincere. It has been a comfort and a source of encouragement and strength to the Christians in Rome and to all Christians since then. Take Mark's example to heart. The Church needs you. The need for evangelists, those who are willing to share the good news with others, is still very real.

Tell a story or lesson that you have been taught and that you will remember.

How will you evangelize? How will you share the good news with others?

Scripture

As Catholics we believe the Holy Spirit speaks to us through Scripture. Take time this week to read the following passage. Reflect on the gifts the Holy Spirit has given you.

Now there are varieties of gifts, but the same Spirit; and there are varieties of services, but the same Lord; and there are varieties of activities, but it is the same God who activates all of them in everyone. To each is given the manifestation of the Spirit for the common good. To one is given through the Spirit the utterance of wisdom, and to another the utterance of knowledge according to the same Spirit, to another faith by the same Spirit, to another gifts of healing by the one Spirit, to another the working of miracles, to another prophecy, to another the discernment of spirits, to another various kinds of tongues, to another the interpretation of tongues. All these are activated by one and the same Spirit, who allots to each one individually just as the Spirit chooses (1 Corinthians 12:4–11).

Language of Faith

Divine inspiration   The authors of Scripture were moved and guided by the Holy Spirit. The Bible is truly God's word, spoken in the words of humans.

Literal interpretation   The first step in the study of Scripture requires knowing what the words mean. This is the literal interpretation.

Contextual interpretation   To understand the way words are used in Scripture, scholars study the history and culture of the writer and the people of the times. The meaning of the words in their literary, historical, and cultural framework is the contextual interpretation.

Old Testament   The first part of the Bible tells the story of the Jewish people before Jesus was born. It is made up of the Pentateuch, or Torah, the prophetic books, and other writings, such as religious histories and wisdom literature.

New Testament   The second part of the Bible contains the story of Jesus and his followers. It contains the four Gospels, an account of the early Church, a number of letters, and the Book of Revelation.

THE HOLY SPIRIT IN OUR LIVES

Life Map

1. Key People

List the names of two or three people other than your parents who are very important to you at this point in your life. Be prepared to say why these individuals are important to you.

4. Obstacles Along The Way

Describe, in words or symbols, one failure or disappointment you have experienced in the last year.

Describe in words or symbols one or two events that have made a lasting impression on you.

2. Significant Events

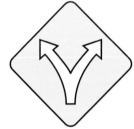

5. Future Directions And Goals

List one or two goals you have for your future.

3. Accomplishments

Describe, in words or symbols, one or two accomplishments that you are especially proud of having achieved in the last six to twelve months.

How has your faith life changed as a result of the people, events, accomplishments, and obstacles that you have met or faced?

Visualizing Your Faith

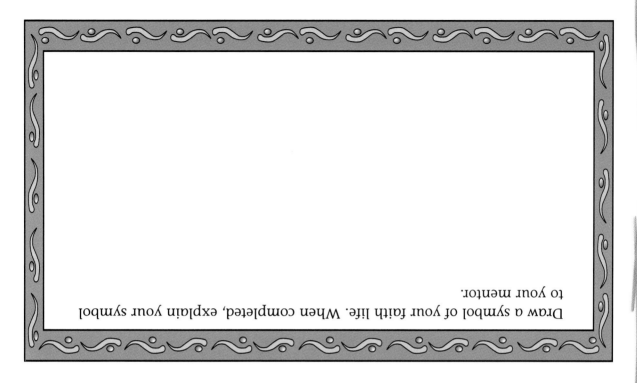

Draw a symbol of your faith life. When completed, explain your symbol to your mentor.

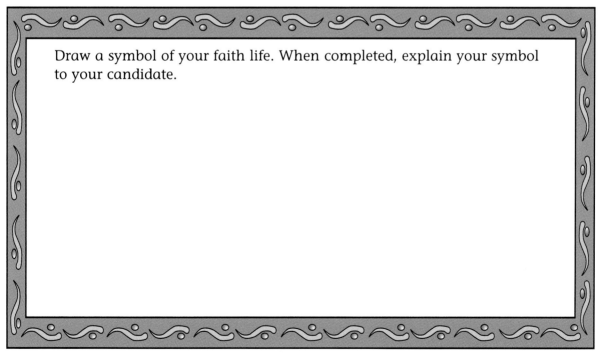

Draw a symbol of your faith life. When completed, explain your symbol to your candidate.

Catholic Beliefs

A Gift

When you have faith in a person, faith in your friends, or faith in your family, you trust that person or persons. When you have faith in God, you have that same kind of trust. Faith, according to the *Catechism of the Catholic Church*, "is a personal act—the free response of the human person to the initiative of God who reveals himself" (166). It is first and foremost a gift (50, 153), the gift of an ongoing relationship between the individual and the divine (52, 142). That gift is characterized by a deep and radical trust (154). Many theologians would say that within you, at the core of your being, lies a longing for this relationship (27). Saint Augustine put it well, saying: "My soul will not be at rest, until it rests in God."

Personal Relationship

Each person has a very personal and unique relationship with God. The Holy Spirit speaks within the context of this personal relationship. As your faith continues to deepen, you understand and see things from a new viewpoint. You feel even more connected to God and to his plan for you and for the world. This is what the Sacraments of Initiation together celebrate—the new connections and deepening bonds.

Community Relationship

Faith is a deeply personal act, but it is not an isolated act. Underscoring the relational dimension of faith, you come to understand that you cannot believe alone. As Christians who profess a belief in the Triune God, you are called to be in relationship not only with God, but with others and with all of creation. The *Catechism of the Catholic Church* uses the image of links in a chain (166), each believer bound to another, called not only to receive the gift of faith, but to pass it on to others. Being part of a faith community means connecting with the ideas and feelings of others.

Seeing and Hearing

As a believer, you are called to see with the eyes of faith and hear with the ears of faith. When you see and hear in this way, you discover new possibilities, you recognize new strengths and talents. You see the world in a totally different way. Not unlike the disciples in the Pentecost story, you will find yourself able to do things you never thought possible and to relate to people in new ways.

A New Name

One element of the new language of faith may be a new name. Often when something significant happens in a person's life, he or she is given a new name. One such example is when a person earns a special degree or honor; a title is added to the person's name.

Confirmation Names

You are asked to begin thinking about your Confirmation name and how you will use this ritual to help integrate your identity as a fully initiated member of the Catholic Church. You have a choice to keep your baptismal name, signifying that you are confirming the faith that was given to you at your Baptism. You may also choose to add a name, to signify your new and deeper awareness of what it means to be a disciple of Jesus. If the choice is made to add a new name, it is to be a Christian name. It should reflect a saint whom you can admire and imitate.

Fruits of the Holy Spirit

Charity (Love)—the highest form of Christian love, directed toward God and our neighbors

Joy—the confident happiness and hope resulting from charity

Peace—the inner harmony that comes from living in charity

Patience—the ability to cope with trying circumstances without becoming bitter

Kindness—the sympathy and affection we show toward others

Goodness—the desire for virtue and not evil

Faithfulness—the loyalty paid to our relationships and beliefs, and first of all to God

Modesty—respectful dress, speech, and conduct toward others

Chastity—living God's gift of sexuality appropriately, according to our state in life

Gentleness—the ability to act tenderly

Generosity—the opposite of selfishness, giving freely

Self-control—the discipline to use our human freedom responsibly

Scripture

By contrast, the fruit of the Spirit is love, joy, peace, patience, kindness, generosity, faithfulness, gentleness, and self-control (Galatians 5:22–23).

What's In a Name?

Questions for the candidate.

Find out what your name means. Write the meaning of your name below.

Ask your parents to tell you the story of how they chose your name. In two or three sentences summarize the story in the space below.

List the name or names you are currently considering for your Confirmation name.

Questions for the mentor.

Find out what your name means. Write the meaning of your name below.

What name did you choose for your Confirmation name?

Explain your reason for choosing this name.

The Little Way

Marie Francoise Thérèse Martin (more commonly referred to as Saint Thérèse of Lisieux) was born on January 2, 1873, in Alencon, France. She was the youngest of five girls. The Martin family lived a comfortable, secure, middle-class life. They encouraged their children to live holy lives in the world. This insight, that holiness was not only desirable but possible, profoundly influenced Thérèse's understanding of faith.

When Thérèse was four years old, her mother died. The Martins moved to the town of Lisieux to be near relatives. In Lisieux there was a Carmelite convent. One by one her sisters became Carmelite nuns. At age fifteen Thérèse followed.

Despite the strict life of the convent, Thérèse thrived. Her sense of humor and gentle spirit were a delight to all the other nuns. Thérèse took great pleasure in all the small ordinary things in life. In gratitude for all God's gifts, Thérèse was constantly, "doing little favors for God" by doing little favors for others. Thérèse believed that you didn't have to be important to be holy, you only had to live life to the fullest, appreciating everything God gave you, and responding with simple kindness. Thérèse referred to this as her "little way."

In her early twenties Thérèse contracted tuberculosis. There was no cure. She suffered terribly but bravely clung to her belief in the "little way." Throughout her illness, she continued to do her little favors for God and to look for the joy in the simple ordinary things of life. She died at the age of twenty-four.

—Newland, Mary Reed. *The Saint Book.* New York: The Seabury Press, 1979.

—Coulson, John, ed. *The Saints: A Concise Biographical Dictionary.* New York: Hawthorn Books, Inc., 1958.

—Farmer, David Hugh, ed. *Butler's Lives of the Saints.* Collegeville, MN: The Liturgical Press, 1996.

Thérèse lived a pretty uneventful life, but she lived it well, appreciating everything and everyone. Pope John Paul II declared her a Doctor of the Church, a title reserved for the great teachers in the Church. The Spirit works in mysterious ways, but often in the simple, the ordinary, the everyday.

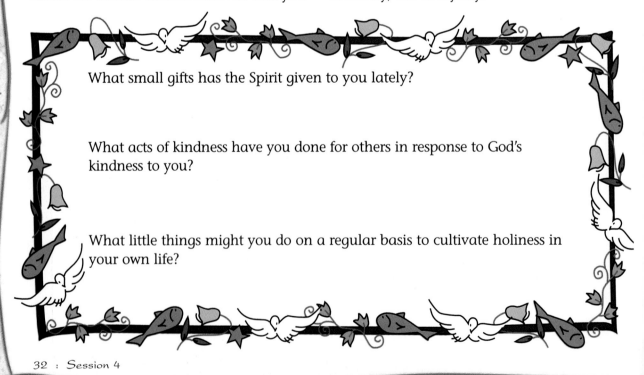

What small gifts has the Spirit given to you lately?

What acts of kindness have you done for others in response to God's kindness to you?

What little things might you do on a regular basis to cultivate holiness in your own life?

Scripture

"I am God Almighty; . . . As for me, this is my covenant with you: You shall be the ancestor of a multitude of nations. No longer shall your name be Abram, but your name shall be Abraham; for I have made you the ancestor of a multitude of nations" (Genesis 17:1–5).

God said to Abraham, "As for Sarai your wife, you shall not call her Sarai, but Sarah shall be her name. I will bless her, and moreover I will give you a son by her. I will bless her, and she shall give rise to nations; kings of peoples shall come from her" (Genesis 17:15–16).

When they came to the crowd, a man came to him, knelt before him, and said, "Lord, have mercy on my son, for he is an epileptic and he suffers terribly; he often falls into the fire and often into the water. And I brought him to your disciples, but they could not cure him." . . . And Jesus rebuked the demon, and it came out of him, and the boy was cured instantly. Then the disciples came to Jesus privately and said, "Why could we not cast it out?" He said to them, "Because of your little faith. For truly I tell you, if you have faith the size of a mustard seed, you will say to this mountain, 'Move from here to there,' and it will move; and nothing will be impossible for you" (Matthew 17:14–20).

Language of Faith

Holy Spirit   The third Person of the Trinity, known as the paraclete, is the energizing power of God's love in our lives. The Spirit proceeds from the Father and the Son and is sent by Christ to the Church as an advocate and guide. Through Baptism the Holy Spirit makes us all one body in Christ. Through Confirmation we receive an increase in the gifts of the Spirit to strengthen us to live as disciples of Jesus. Eucharist nourishes us so that, united to Christ and one another, we can continue Jesus' work in the world.

Faith   Each person's awareness of his or her personal relationship with God, based on trust, and his or her response to that relationship. Christian faith is a person's awareness of and response to God through their relationship with Jesus Christ. The virtue that helps us believe in God and in all that he has revealed to us.

Faith community   A group of people who share a similar understanding of God's relationship with them. Catholics share a belief in the risen Jesus and his message, which they express through membership in the community of the Catholic Church.

BAPTISMAL PROMISES

Baptismal Promises

Do you reject Satan and all his works and all his empty promises?
Candidates: *I do.*

Do you believe in God the Father Almighty, creator of heaven and earth?
Candidates: *I do.*

Do you believe in Jesus Christ, his only Son, our Lord,
who was born of the Virgin Mary,
was crucified, died, and was buried,
rose from the dead,
and is now seated at the right hand of the Father?
Candidates: *I do.*

Do you believe in the Holy Spirit,
the Lord, the giver of life,
who came upon the apostles at Pentecost
and will be given to you sacramentally in Confirmation?
Candidates: *I do.*

Do you believe in the holy catholic Church,
the communion of saints, the forgiveness of sins,
the resurrection of the body, and life everlasting?
Candidates: *I do.*

This is our faith. This is the faith of the Church.
We are proud to profess it in Christ Jesus our Lord.
Amen.

—*The Rites*, "Confirmation Renewal of Baptismal Promises," #23.

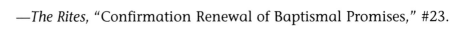

Reflections on Renewing My Baptismal Vows

Why do you think it is important to have people renew these promises?

Which of the baptismal promises, if any, did you find difficult to make?

What did you find most prayerful or moving in the liturgy during which you renewed your baptismal promises?

Questions for the candidate.

Questions for the mentor.

What did you find most prayerful or moving in the liturgy during which you renewed your baptismal promises?

Which of the baptismal promises, if any, did you find difficult to make?

Why do you think it is important to have people renew these promises?

Catholic Beliefs

Service

Service is an essential part of the Christian life. Through your baptismal promises, you were asked to carry on the work and ministry of Jesus. By virtue of your Baptism, you were called to "share in the priesthood of Christ, in his prophetic and royal mission" (CCC, 1268). Baptism both grants the rights of the priesthood to all believers and demands that we live out this priesthood responsibility.

Gifts from the Spirit

The Spirit confers on each baptized person the gifts needed to carry on the ministry of Jesus. These gifts are to be used for the common good. Common good assumes a respect and dignity for the human person and for those things needed for a truly human life: food, clothing, health, education (CCC, 1908). A variety of gifts are given to the Christian community through individual members. A good summary of these gifts can be found in 1 Corinthians 12:4–11.

Responsibility of Each Member

The Church sees ministry or service as the responsibility of each member of the faith community (CCC, 909). Baptism gives us new life. In the Eucharist we are nourished with Jesus' Body and Blood (CCC, 1275). Through Confirmation the baptized are enriched with the special strength of the Holy Spirit to witness and defend the faith through word and action (CCC, 1285). Jesus himself showed us what it means to be a servant and to minister to those in need.

Service as a Gift

Too often, service is seen by many as either "a nice thing to do" or a chore. Yet if given the chance, young people usually respond with gifts of generosity and optimism. And young people have a sixth sense when it comes to injustice. Herein lies your most prophetic witness. "That's not fair" could be your mantra! What is needed for initiating service is guidance in forming a social conscience that allows you to see more clearly and more readily the needs of others. You are encouraged to help those who hunger and thirst for justice (CCC, 1928, 1932).

Service Can Make a Difference

A man spoke with the Lord about heaven and hell. The Lord said to the man, "Come, I will show you hell." They entered a room where a group of people sat around a huge pot of stew. Everyone was famished, desperate and starving. Each held a spoon that reached the pot, but each spoon had a handle so much longer than the person's own arm that it could not be used to get the stew into his or her own mouth. The suffering was terrible.

"Come, now I will show you heaven," the Lord said after a while. They entered another room, identical to the first—the pot of stew, the group of people, the same long-handled spoons. But there everyone was happy and well-nourished.

"I don't understand," said the man. "Why are they happy here when they were miserable in the other room and everything was the same?"

The Lord smiled. "Ah, it is simple," he said. "Here they have learned to feed one another."

Personal Qualities

Directions: Circle the qualities or talents you see in yourself. When finished, have your mentor place an asterisk in front of the qualities he or she sees in you. Discuss any differences.

Active	Helpful	Reliable
Amusing	Honest	Religious
Appreciative	Intelligent	Responsible
Artistic	Interesting	Self-confident
Athletic	Jocular	Sensible
Brave	Just	Sincere
Bright	Kind	Steadfast
Caring	Levelheaded	Strong
Considerate	Loyal	Supportive
Cooperative	Neat	Talkative
Creative	Nice	Tenacious
Decisive	Observant	Thoughtful
Dependable	Open-minded	Tolerant
Easygoing	Peacemaker	Trustworthy
Energetic	Persistent	Understanding
Fair	Personable	Unique
Friendly	Questioning	Warm
Fun	Quick-witted	Welcoming
Generous	Quiet	Well-adjusted
Gregarious	Reflective	

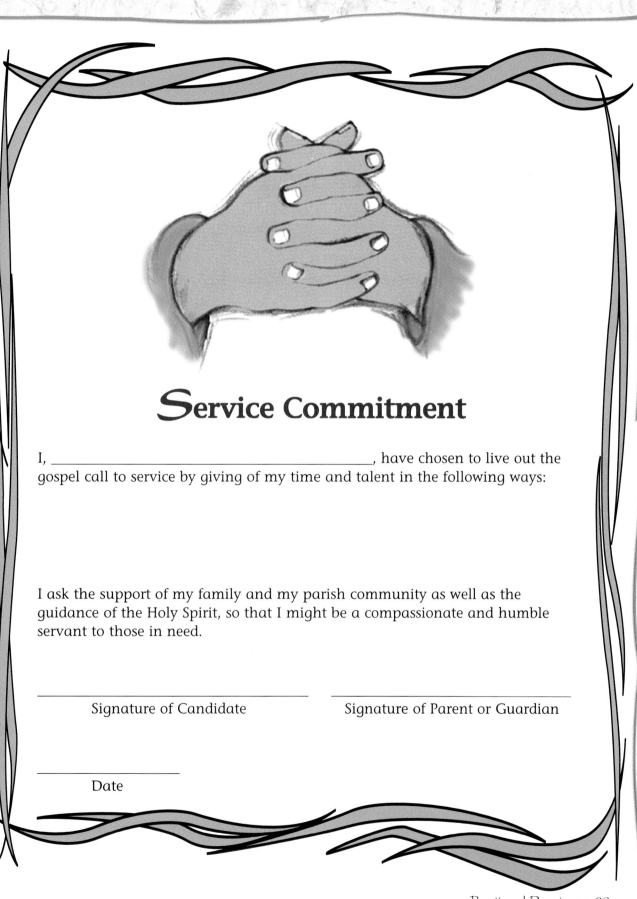

Service Commitment

I, _____, have chosen to live out the gospel call to service by giving of my time and talent in the following ways:

I ask the support of my family and my parish community as well as the guidance of the Holy Spirit, so that I might be a compassionate and humble servant to those in need.

_____   _____
Signature of Candidate   Signature of Parent or Guardian

_____
Date

A Royal Servant

Elizabeth was born in 1207 to the King and Queen of Hungary. At age four her father promised her in marriage to Ludwig IV, whom she married when she was fourteen. Though the marriage was arranged for political reasons, their relationship was characterized by genuine affection and respect.

Elizabeth was an independent woman and had a fierce devotion to people who were poor. It was expected that a woman in Elizabeth's position would be generous to those who were poor, but Elizabeth's generosity extended to giving away much of her fortune. She was often seen begging in the streets on behalf of those who were poor, and she founded and administered a hospital for them. Such activity was seen as outrageous. But even more than her unconventional behavior, Elizabeth was hated by those who were rich and powerful because she dared to say that the poor were poor because the rich were too rich. She herself began to fast, eating only food that had been justly acquired.

After four years of marriage and three children, Ludwig died. Immediately his family sought to put a stop to Elizabeth's excessive charity and unusual practices.

Her brother-in-law sought to force-feed Elizabeth. They forbade her to beg in the streets or work in the hospital she founded. When she continued to act against their wishes, Ludwig's family claimed she was crazy. They took away her right to the family fortune and assumed custody of her children. Penniless and disgraced, Elizabeth went into the streets as a poor woman, living at the hospital she founded. She died at the age of twenty-four. She is remembered as a true disciple of Jesus, a model Christian, a heroine, a saint.

—Fiorenza, Elizabeth Schüssler. *Discipleship of Equals: A Critical Feminist Ekklesia-logy of Liberation.* New York: The Crossroad Publishing Co., 1993.

Elizabeth's story is sad, but it is also an inspiring story. Working for justice is difficult. People who are called to reform their lives are not always willing to do so. Furthermore, they often blame and ridicule the people who point out the injustice. We have all seen what happens when someone sticks up for someone who is less than popular. Pretty soon the "in crowd" makes sure that you get the message—hang out with her or him and you are no longer one of us. Such social pressure often works, and the injustice continues. Take heart from Elizabeth's story. Everyone is called to work for peace and justice.

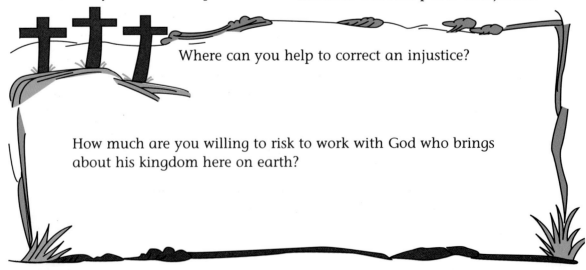

Where can you help to correct an injustice?

How much are you willing to risk to work with God who brings about his kingdom here on earth?

Scripture

John answered all of them by saying, "I baptize you with water; but one who is more powerful than I is coming; I am not worthy to untie the thong of his sandals. He will baptize you with the Holy Spirit and fire" (Luke 3:16).

Is not this the fast that I choose:
to loose the bonds of injustice,
to undo the thongs of the yoke,
to let the oppressed go free,
and to break every yoke?
Is it not to share your bread with the hungry,
and bring the homeless poor into your house;
when you see the naked, to cover them,
and not to hide yourself from your own kin?
Then your light shall break forth like the dawn,
and your healing shall spring up quickly;
your vindicator shall go before you,
the glory of the LORD shall be your rear guard.
(Isaiah 58:6–8)

Language of Faith

Baptismal promises   The baptized person promises to reject Satan and all his works and all his empty promises and to assent to the beliefs stated in the Apostles' Creeds. When infants are baptized, their parents and godparents witness to their own faith by renewing their own baptismal promises.

Service   Actions that help to meet the needs of others by using our God-given abilities and talents. Most often Christian service is identified with the Corporal Works of Mercy—feed the hungry, clothe the naked, give drink to the thirsty, shelter the homeless, tend the sick, visit those in prison, and bury the dead.

Gifts of the Holy Spirit   These are the special insights and abilities bestowed by God on the Church and on all members who are confirmed which enable them to carry out the mission of Jesus in the world. The gifts of the Spirit, conferred during Confirmation, are wisdom, understanding, knowledge, courage (fortitude), reverence (piety), right judgment (counsel), and wonder and awe in God's presence (fear of the Lord).

Rite of sprinkling   A ritual in which the assembled members of the faith community are blessed with a sprinkling of holy water to remind them of their Baptism.

THE LAYING ON OF HANDS

Traditions of the Liturgical Seasons

Directions: Circle the traditions that your parish or family participates in during the seasons listed. Add any additional traditions that your family has.

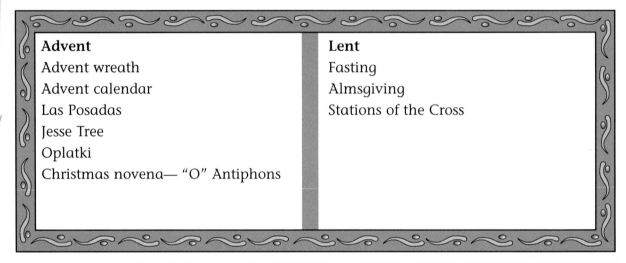

Advent
Advent wreath
Advent calendar
Las Posadas
Jesse Tree
Oplatki
Christmas novena— "O" Antiphons

Lent
Fasting
Almsgiving
Stations of the Cross

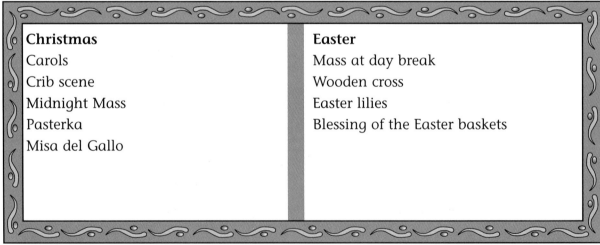

Christmas
Carols
Crib scene
Midnight Mass
Pasterka
Misa del Gallo

Easter
Mass at day break
Wooden cross
Easter lilies
Blessing of the Easter baskets

If your family doesn't have ways of celebrating religious traditions, how do you feel about that?

Apostolic and Ecclesial Traditions of the Catholic Church

On the line below place a capital "T" in front of those traditions of the Church you believe are Apostolic Traditions and cannot be fundamentally changed. Place a lowercase "t" in front of those traditions you believe are ecclesial traditions and can be changed.

_____ Jesus is the Son of God.

_____ The way Communion is distributed

_____ Mary is the Mother of God.

_____ Fasting regulations

_____ The resurrection

_____ Papal infallibility

_____ Catholic teaching on capital punishment

_____ Holy days of obligation

_____ The Apostles' Creed

_____ The liturgical calendar

_____ The books chosen to be in the Bible

_____ The prayers said at Mass

_____ The boundaries of Vatican City

_____ The existence of hell

Catholic Beliefs

Tradition and Scripture

Tradition and Scripture are bound closely together and communicate with one another. Each of them makes present and fruitful in the Church the mystery of Christ (CCC, 80). Both must be accepted and honored with equal sentiments of devotion and reverence (CCC, 82).

Apostolic Traditions

The Church differentiates between *Apostolic Traditions* and *ecclesial traditions*. Scripture and Apostolic Traditions contain the "sacred deposit" of faith. Church doctrines guide us in our understanding of God and his plan for us. Our belief in the Trinity, in Mary as the Virgin Mother of God, and the Real Presence of Christ in the Eucharist are all examples of scriptural Apostolic Traditions that are doctrine. Apostolic Tradition is found in the Apostles' Creed, the Nicene Creed, and the Councils of the Church. These Traditions cannot be fundamentally changed, for they have been divinely ordained and the entire people of God are asked to adhere faithfully to these teachings (CCC, 84).

Ecclesial Traditions

Ecclesial traditions refer to customs and practices that developed in local churches for particular reasons in a given time and place. These traditions can be maintained, changed, or even dropped under the guidance of the Holy Spirit through the pope and other bishops (CCC, 83). Examples of ecclesial traditions are kneeling or standing during specific parts of the Mass, the color of Mass vestments, the choice of readings proclaimed at Mass, and so on.

Prayer Traditions

One element that incorporates both Apostolic and ecclesial traditions is in the area of prayer. When praying, we can use prayers that have been used by Christians since the Middle Ages such as the Rosary, or earlier, such as the Lord's Prayer and the Apostles' Creed. The traditions of our Church provide for private or individual prayer, shared prayer, and liturgical prayer. Praying the Rosary and reading Scripture with a group of people are examples of shared prayer. Mass and the celebration of the sacraments are examples of liturgical prayer.

Use of Symbols in Tradition

There are many symbols used in our faith tradition, such as the Bible or Lectionary, which symbolize the role of Scripture in prayer, certain colors, which indicate the various liturgical seasons in our Catholic tradition, and green plants, which symbolize new life. One of the most important symbols in our traditions is the Paschal or Easter candle.

Ritual Traditions

The laying on of hands is an ancient symbol. In the Hebrew faith, hands were laid on prophets and kings as a sign of God's favor and as a symbol of both blessing and commissioning. In the early Church the apostles imparted the gift of the Spirit by laying hands on the newly baptized. This ritual gesture is seen in the Catholic tradition as the origin of the Sacrament of Confirmation. In the celebration of Confirmation, the bishop and the priests present for the celebration will lay, or impose, hands on you while the bishop prays that the Spirit be sent to you.

Prayer Traditions

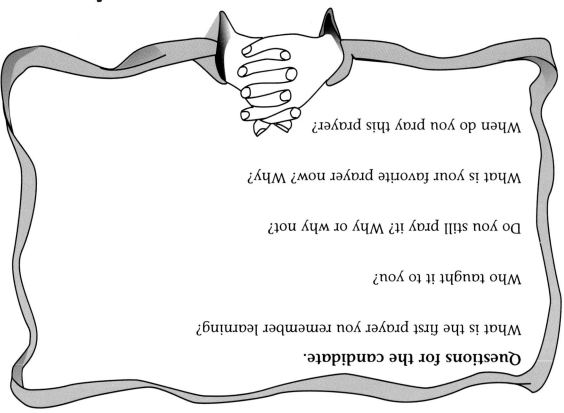

Questions for the candidate.

What is the first prayer you remember learning?

Who taught it to you?

Do you still pray it? Why or why not?

What is your favorite prayer now? Why?

When do you pray this prayer?

Questions for the mentor.

What is the first prayer that you remember learning?

Who taught it to you?

Do you still pray it? Why or why not?

What is your favorite prayer now? Why?

When do you pray this prayer?

Come, Holy Spirit

Directions: Use the space below to write a prayer to the Holy Spirit. Reflect on what it is that you want the Holy Spirit to do for you as you prepare for Confirmation. Try to use all five forms of prayer—blessing and adoration of God, petition for oneself, thanksgiving to God, intercession for others, and praise of God.

Rooted in Prayer and Tradition

Hildegard of Bingen was born in the year 1098. She came from a large family who lived in a densely forested area of what is now southern Germany. By all accounts she was a joyful child, full of curiosity and optimism. She loved nature.

As a young child, Hildegard was sent to live with Jutta, a well-known spiritual teacher in the area. Under Jutta's guardianship Hildegard grew up to be quite a remarkable person. Jutta taught Hildegard about prayer and instilled in her an even deeper appreciation for God's creation.

As a young adult, Hildegard became a Benedictine nun. As a Benedictine she prayed seven times a day with the other sisters. As a result of her prayer, she had visions and vivid dreams that helped her know what God wanted from her and others. She urged all people, but especially those in authority, to be faithful to the traditions of the Church and the will of God. She was a prophetic voice at a time when many had lost sight of their moral and spiritual values.

Hildegard lived to be eighty years old. During her life she gained the admiration and respect of many. Most importantly, she remained true to herself and her beliefs. She rooted her life in prayer and in the traditions of the Church.

—Coulson, John ed. *The Saints: A Concise Biographical Dictionary*. New York: Hawthorn Books, Inc., 1958.

—Attwater, Donald. *The Avenel Dictionary of Saints*. New York: Avenel Books, 1981.

—Greene, Carol. *Beggars, Beasts and Easter Fire Stories of Early Saints*. Batiavia, IL: Lion Publishing, 1993.

What might we learn from Hildegard's example?

How might you pray more creatively through nature? Music? Community? Symbols? Silence?

Scripture

"But whenever you pray, go into your room and shut the door and pray to your Father who is in secret; and your Father who sees in secret will reward you.

When you are praying, do not heap up empty phrases as the Gentiles do; for they think that they will be heard because of their many words. Do not be like them, for your Father knows what you need before you ask him" (Matthew 6:6–8).

Then little children were being brought to him in order that he might lay his hands on them and pray. The disciples spoke sternly to those who brought them; but Jesus said, "Let the little children come to me, and do not stop them; for it is to such as these that the kingdom of heaven belongs." And he laid his hands on them and went on his way (Matthew 19:13–15).

Language of Faith

Apostolic Tradition The teachings the apostles handed on to us from what they learned from Jesus' teaching and example and under the guidance of the Holy Spirit, as accepted in the belief, practice, and teaching of the Church.

Ecclesial tradition The bishops, exercising the teaching office in the Church, develop certain teachings and practices to assist the whole people of God in their pursuit of holiness and virtue. These practices respond to the needs of people in different cultures and different times and can be changed, amended, and even abandoned.

Prayer "The raising of one's mind and heart to God or the requesting of good things from God" (CCC, 2644). Prayer is categorized in five different forms: adoration and blessing, petition, intercession, thanksgiving, and praise. We can pray as individuals (private prayer), in common with others (shared prayer), or publicly in union with the whole Church (liturgical prayer).

Laying on of Hands (Imposition of Hands) During the Sacraments of Baptism, Confirmation, and Holy Orders, the priest or bishop places his hands on the head or touches in a solemn manner the body of the person receiving the sacrament. This is an ancient tradition. The apostles were said to confer the gift of the Holy Spirit by laying their hands on people.

ANOINTING

Objects Used in Prayer

All the objects mentioned below can be included in a prayer service or in the reception of a sacrament. Match the objects with their symbolism or use.

Name

1. ____ ambo or pulpit

2. ____ Scripture

3. ____ Paschal candle

4. ____ candles

5. ____ music

6. ____ burning of incense

7. ____ red

8. ____ green

9. ____ white

10. ____ purple

11. ____ chrism

12. ____ oil of catechumens

13. ____ oil of the sick

14. ____ crucifix

15. ____ holy water

Symbolism or Use

a. people and holy objects are venerated with this

b. oil used in Baptism, Confirmation, and Holy Orders

c. serves as a focal point for Liturgy of the Word

d. one of the many symbols that can express Christ's presence

e. symbolizes the Holy Spirit; color worn by the presider for Confirmation

f. used for baptizing and blessing

g. oil used in the Sacrament of the Anointing of the Sick

h. the word of God read during prayer

i. used to praise God in song

j. symbolizes new life

k. a prime Christ, Easter, or resurrection symbol

l. symbolizes growth

m. symbolizes repentance

n. symbol of Jesus' suffering

o. first oil used during Baptism

The Paschal Candle

During the Easter Vigil the Paschal candle is inscribed as follows:

Movement	Prayer to be said with each movement
A vertical bar from A to Ω	Christ yesterday and today,
A horizontal cross bar	the beginning and the end.
The Alpha	Alpha
The Omega	and Omega;
The "2"	all time belongs to him
The "0"	and all the ages;
The "0"	to him be glory and power,
The "0"	through every age forever.

After inscribing the candle, the celebrant may insert five grains of incense held in place by red wax nails. He says the following as he inserts each nail:

nail 1	By his holy
nail 2	and glorious wounds
nail 3	may Christ our Lord
nail 4	guard us
nail 5	and keep us. Amen.

The celebrant lights the candle from the new fire praying, "May the Light of Christ, rising in glory, dispel the darkness of our hearts and minds."

Catholic Beliefs

Paschal Candle

The new Paschal candle is lit for the first time at the Easter Vigil on Holy Saturday. The celebrant marks the candle with the cross, the first and last letters of the Greek alphabet, and the date of the present year. Five grains of incense are inserted in the form of the cross, representing the five wounds of Christ. It is placed in a prominent place near the ambo and lit at each Mass from Easter through Pentecost, when it moved to a less prominent place near the baptismal font. The candle is lit and used at Baptisms and funerals as a symbol of new life in Christ.

Incense

The rising smoke and fragrance of incense is an acceptable prayer. *"Let my prayer be counted as incense before you, and the lifting up of my hands as an evening sacrifice"* (Psalm 141:2). Incense is used to venerate the gathered assembly at Mass and the body of the deceased during a funeral. Holy objects that can be incensed are the altar, the Paschal candle, the Book of the Gospels, and the gifts of bread and wine.

Colors

Certain colors are associated with liturgical feasts or seasons. White is used during the Easter and Christmas Seasons, to mark special Marian feasts, and at weddings, and funerals. Purple is used during the Lenten and Advent Seasons. Red is used to symbolize the Holy Spirit or to mark feast days of martyrs. The most commonly used color is green, which marks Ordinary Time.

Oils

The blessing of the oils is traditionally done by a bishop on Holy Thursday. Each local parish is then given a small supply of each of the following: oil of the catechumens, chrism, and oil of the sick. In Baptism we are anointed with sacred chrism, signifying the gift of the Holy Spirit. Chrism is an effective sign that Baptism incorporates us into Christ, who is anointed priest, prophet, and king. Chrism is made from a mixture of olive oil and balsam. The oil of the catechumens may also be used in the celebration of Baptism as part of the exorcisms when we renounce Satan (CCC, 1237).

Anointing with sacred chrism also takes place in the Sacrament of Confirmation. This second anointing, conferred by the bishop, confirms and completes the anointing at Baptism (CCC, 1241–1242). Incorporated into Christ who is priest, prophet, and king, Christians are called to renounce evil and embrace God's call to service.

This call to service is again acknowledged sacramentally in Holy Orders. The anointing with sacred chrism is given as an effective sign of the Holy Spirit's presence and promise in making the ministry of the ordained fruitful (CCC, 1574).

The oil of the sick is used only during the Sacrament of the Anointing of the Sick. Through the anointing the Holy Spirit confers the gifts of strength, peace, and courage in the face of serious illness or the frailty of old age or death (CCC, 1520).

Anointing

Throughout Scripture we find examples of anointings—David, Solomon, and Isaiah, to name a few. The preeminent example, of course, is Jesus, who is the "anointed one of God." This rite was believed to confer strength, wisdom, and courage and was used to designate God's chosen servants. The anointing with oil in the Rite of Confirmation symbolizes selection and strength, as it did in biblical times (CCC, 1293). It has also become synonymous with the Holy Spirit (CCC, 695).

During the Sacrament of Confirmation, the bishop or presider says, *"N., be sealed with the Gift of the Holy Spirit,"* as he makes a sign of the cross on the forehead of each candidate. "By this anointing the confirmand receives the 'mark,' the seal of the Holy Spirit. A seal is a symbol of a person, a sign of personal authority, or ownership of an object" [Cf. *Gen* 38:18; 41:42; *Deut* 32:34; *CT* 8:6] (CCC, 1295). This is similar to a presidential seal used to authenticate a document or the Good Housekeeping seal to symbolize approval. Being marked with the sign of the cross is a reminder that we share in the life of Christ (CCC, 265). The "Amen" response by the candidates is their personal affirmation of their desire to witness to Christ in the world (CCC, 1064).

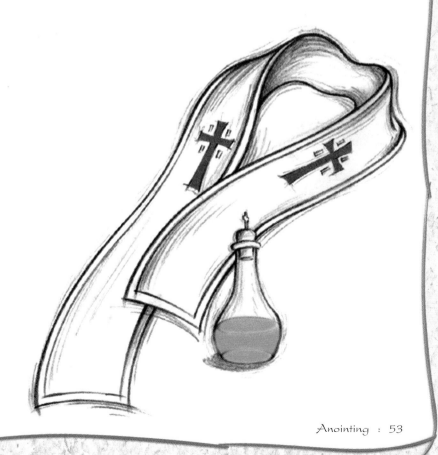

What Helps Me Pray

Questions for the candidate.

What object used in prayer had you not noticed or paid much attention to before?

How did knowing the symbolism or use of this object add to the prayer experience?

What did it feel like to be blessed?

As the bishop or celebrant anoints your forehead during the Sacrament of Confirmation, he says: *N., be sealed with the Gift of the Holy Spirit.* What meaning will this have for you?

Questions for the mentor.

What object used in prayer had you not noticed or paid much attention to before?

How did knowing the symbolism or use of this object add to the prayer experience?

Vocabulary Crossword Puzzle

Across

4. Coming directly from the apostles
8. Those seeking identity with Christ and membership in the Church
9. Raising one's mind and heart to God
15. Sacrament that seals us with the Holy Spirit
16. Another word for love
19. Third Person of the Trinity
21. To rub or mark with oil
23. Cleansing ritual

Down

1. Personal response to our relationship with God
2. To rejoice; state of great happiness or delight
3. Collection of books divinely inspired by God
5. A summary of Jesus' path to the kingdom

6. First sacrament of initiation
7. Process whereby we reestablish or build up a relationship damaged by sin
8. A sacred promise or agreement made between two parties
10. Used for anointing in the Sacraments of Baptism, Confirmation, and Holy Orders
11. Helping meet the needs of others
12. Right and responsibility of all the baptized
13. The liturgical traditions or celebrations of the Church
14. The quality of being humble and not pretentious
17. Motivated by God
18. The formal public prayer of the Church
20. To be chosen in the biblical sense
22. To disobey God

The Woman Who Anointed Jesus

Luke tells the story of an encounter Jesus has with a woman in the house of Simon the Pharisee. We are told that Simon invited Jesus to his home, that Jesus accepted the invitation, and that while having dinner, Jesus encountered an unusual woman.

While Jesus was eating at Simon's house, a woman, known to the local people and presumably to Simon's guests as a sinner, enters and stands behind Jesus. She weeps and her tears fall upon the feet of Jesus. She then dries his feet with her hair and anoints them with perfumed oil. Simon is outraged. Who does she think she is, coming into his house and treating a guest of his in such a manner? Does Jesus know of her reputation? Jesus reminds Simon that it is a customary sign of hospitality and respect for a guest that a host provide water for guests to wash their feet. Simon did not offer this simple act of hospitality to Jesus, so who was he to criticize the woman? Who is Simon to judge? Simon does not answer.

But it is not only Simon who criticizes the woman. Jesus' disciples judge her harshly, accusing her of wasting precious oil that could have been used to support those who are poor. Jesus rebukes them as well. Who are they to judge? Then Jesus reminds all who are present that love and forgiveness are important values in God the Father's kingdom. The woman was not perfect, but she reached out in love. Jesus knew her sinfulness, but chose instead to look with kindness upon her and see not the wrong she did but the act of love and kindness she offered another human.

—Newland, Mary Reed. *The Saint Book.*
New York: The Seabury Press, 1979.

The woman's act was a simple one. It was ordinary in one sense but full of sincerity and love. When God looks at you what does he see? Will God see an arrogant person like Simon, who feels he has the right to judge others because of his status and place in society? Will God see a blind person, like the disciples, who did not understand that the practical thing to do is not always the right thing to do? Or will God see a person who knows the value of love and forgiveness?

If you were to die tomorrow, how would you be remembered by others? Is this the way you want to be remembered?

Scripture

Samuel took a vial of oil and poured it on [Saul's] head, and kissed him; he said, "The Lord has anointed you ruler over his people Israel. You shall reign over the people of the Lord and you will save them from the hand of their enemies all around. Now this shall be the sign to you that the Lord has anointed you ruler over his heritage" (1 Samuel 10:1).

For in him every one of God's promises is a "Yes." For this reason it is through him that we say the "Amen," to the glory of God. But it is God who establishes us with you in Christ and has anointed us, by putting his seal on us and giving us his Spirit in our hearts as a first installment (2 Corinthians 1:20–22).

Language of Faith

Anoint   Marking or rubbing a person with oil. Anointing is an effective sign of God's friendship and the presence of the Holy Spirit. It also means healing and strengthening. Anointing is part of the Sacraments of Baptism, Confirmation, Anointing of the Sick, and Holy Orders.

Chrism   Sacred oil, made from olive oil and scented with spices. It is used for anointing in the Sacraments of Baptism, Confirmation, and Holy Orders.

Catechumens   Those who are preparing to seek identity with Christ, seeking full membership in the Church. During a formation process of unspecified length, the catechumen studies and prays with two groups: other adults who are also seeking full membership in the Church and members of the faith community who assist the catechumens in their quest.

GO IN PEACE TO LOVE AND SERVE THE LORD

New Discoveries

Questions for the newly confirmed.

Identify one thing you discovered about yourself on the journey.

Name a gift you have recognized in yourself as a result of the journey.

What do you remember best from the celebration of Confirmation?

What do you appreciate more about your faith tradition as a result of the journey?

Questions for the mentor.

Identify one thing you discovered about yourself on the journey.

Name a gift you have recognized in yourself as a result of the journey.

What do you remember best from the celebration of Confirmation?

What do you appreciate more about your faith tradition as a result of the journey?

Expectations of the Newly Confirmed

1. Understands that the journey of faith is an ongoing call to seek God with a sincere heart and willingly commits himself or herself to undertake the journey.

2. Acknowledges the existence of sin and seeks to be reconciled with God and others.

3. Recognizes the importance of Scripture and Tradition as guiding influences in his or her moral and spiritual life.

4. Grows in an appreciation of the presence of God in his or her life and cultivates that appreciation through prayer and reflection.

5. Promises to keep the flame of faith entrusted to him or her burning brightly.

6. Makes a commitment to community worship—participating in Sunday Eucharist and celebrating the Sacrament of Reconciliation frequently.

7. Models what it means to be a follower of Christ in his or her personal moral behavior.

8. Accepts the responsibility to love and serve the Lord by loving and serving others.

Catholic Beliefs

Mystagogy

Christian initiation is accomplished through the Sacraments of Baptism, Confirmation, and Eucharist. Sacramental initiation plunges us into a lifelong relationship with God and his people. Though the rituals of initiation are limited in time and space, they lead us into the much richer and deeper reality of Trinitarian life. As a baptized and confirmed Catholic, you are now called to live no longer for yourself but in Christ (*Catechism of the Catholic Church*, 1269). Freed from the slavery of sin and death, you are now free to live as a disciple of the Risen Christ, heir to the kingdom of God. You are promised the gift of eternal life. This recognition does not happen all at once. The greatness to which you have been called is not obtained in a matter of hours or days or even years. As Paul reminds all of us, we find ourselves looking through a dark glass waiting for the day when we will see clearly. We are not capable of grasping the mystery into which we have been immersed. We spend our lives in prayer and reflection, contemplating that mystery. In other words, the work of mystagogy is always ongoing.

Expectations of the Newly Confirmed

When the journey to Confirmation began, you learned there were certain things expected of you. Refer back to page 6 and read again the expectations that were listed. Now you have been anointed and sealed with the Holy Spirit. There are now different expectations of you as a fully initiated member of Christ's Church. One of those expectations is that you take an active role in the mission of the Church (CCC, 1316).

Ministry

In its document *Renewing the Vision: A Framework for Catholic Youth Ministry*, the National Conference of Catholic Bishops has identified eight components of a comprehensive ministry program for youth. These components are also found in any vibrant parish where fully initiated members are involved, active, concerned, and seeking to grow in their faith.

The components include:

Advocacy—speaking on behalf of various groups—families, those who are poor, those who are elderly, and so forth

Catechesis—the effort of the Church to use sacred Scripture and Tradition to form disciples who are knowledgeable about their faith

Community life—building among the community of believers an environment of love, support, and appreciation of diversity

Justice and service—working for justice, serving those in need, pursuing peace and defending the life, dignity, and rights of all people

Evangelization—inviting people into a deeper relationship with Jesus, the Risen Lord, and empowering them to live as his disciples

Leadership—calling forth, affirming, and empowering the diverse gifts, talents, and abilities of members of the faith community

Pastoral care—compassionate presence and outreach to those who are hurting and in need

Prayer and worship—celebrating and deepening people's relationship with Jesus Christ through communal and liturgical prayer

As a confirmed Catholic you are invited and encouraged to reflect on your personal gifts and on ways the gifts can be used to further the mission of the Church. The Rite of Confirmation has been used as the guide for this faith journey. The final statement the bishop made at the celebration of Confirmation was "Go in peace to love and serve the Lord." Your challenge now becomes one of fulfilling this commitment.

Gifts Given

Thank you
for the gifts you have shared with us
while on the journey.

Spiritual Health Inventory

	A strength	Doing fine	Needs work	A weakness
Makes time daily for personal prayer				
Participates in Sunday Eucharist				
Receives the Sacrament of Reconciliation frequently				
Nurtures a spirit of gratitude and generosity				
Admits to faults and wrongdoing				
Accepts forgiveness and forgives others				
Seeks opportunities for conversion				
Respects the sanctity of life				
Respects and protects the rights of others				
Cultivates a love for justice and a desire for peace				
Studies and prays with Scripture				
Appreciates tradition				
Fosters an awareness of God's presence in creation				
Acts on moral values				
Serves others willingly				

Witnesses of Faith

Catholicism reached central Africa relatively recently. The first Catholic missionaries to arrive in Uganda were the White Fathers in 1879. At first, things went well for the missionaries. They established schools and churches under the protection of a friendly local king named Mtesa. Things changed. A cruel and immoral man named Mwanga came to power. When Mwanga's advisor, Joseph Mkasa, a Christian convert, challenged him about his abusive and brutal behavior toward others, Mwanga had him killed. Mwanga believed that killing Joseph would make the other Christians in his household timid and afraid. The opposite happened. The Christians in the household became more committed to their faith and more outspoken about the injustice and immoral behavior they saw around them.

Charles Lwanga became the king's new steward. He could see what the future held. If he and the other young Christian servants continued to live as Christians, they would be killed. One day the king sent for all his servants. He separated the Christians from the others and demanded that the Christians deny their faith. The fifteen Christians, all under the age of 25, refused, and the king in a fit of rage gave the orders to execute them.

Instead, they spent a short time in prison where they were beaten and starved. Then, afraid of public outcry, Mwanga had Charles and his companions marched to a village thirty-seven miles away. Led by Charles, the oldest of the group, and Kizito, the youngest of the group at thirteen, the African Christians made their way to the village of Namugongo. They were put into bamboo cages and chained to stakes in the ground. It took the executioners seven days to collect enough wood to construct a huge bonfire. On June 3, 1886, the prisoners were led out, stripped, wrapped in reed mats, and thrown onto the fire. The chief executioner, unable to face such a cruel death for his own son, killed him first by striking him on the head. The young martyrs piled high on the pyre died singing hymns and calling out the name of Jesus.

—Newland, Mary Reed. *The Saint Book.* New York: The Seabury Press, 1979.

Charles, Kizito, and the others were young. They must have been afraid. But they were blest with gifts of courage, wisdom, counsel, right judgment, reverence, knowledge, and awe and wonder in God's presence. You have also been blessed by the Spirit. Charles and the Ugandan martyrs were a sign of hope for others.

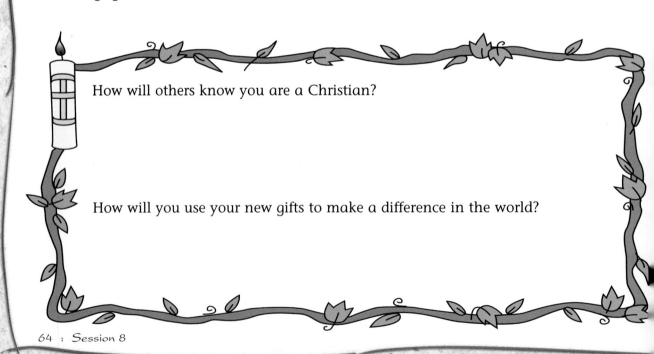

How will others know you are a Christian?

How will you use your new gifts to make a difference in the world?

Scripture

When the day of Pentecost had come, they were all together in one place. And suddenly from heaven there came a sound like the rush of a violent wind, and it filled the entire house where they were sitting. Divided tongues, as of fire, appeared among them, and a tongue rested on each of them. All of them were filled with the Holy Spirit and began to speak in other languages, as the Spirit gave them ability. . . . So those who welcomed his message were baptized, and that day about three thousand persons were added. They devoted themselves to the apostles' teaching and fellowship, to the breaking of bread and the prayers. . . . All who believed were together and had all things in common; they would sell their possessions and goods and distribute the proceeds to all, as any had need. Day by day, as they spent much time together in the temple, they broke bread at home and ate their food with glad and generous hearts, praising God and having the goodwill of all the people. And day by day the Lord added to their number those who were being saved (Acts 2:1–4; 41–42; 44–47).

We declare to you what was from the beginning, what we have heard, what we have seen with our eyes, what we have looked at and touched with our hands, concerning the word of life—this life was revealed, and we have seen it and testify to it, and declare to you the eternal life that was with the Father and was revealed to us—we declare to you what we have seen and heard so that you also may have fellowship with us; and truly our fellowship is with the Father and with his Son Jesus Christ (1 John 1:1–3).

Language of Faith

Mystagogy   The catechesis that has as its goal helping people understand the mysteries of Christ by moving from what is visible to what is invisible. It is the ongoing process of study and reflection by all who have celebrated the Sacraments of Initiation (Baptism, Eucharist, Confirmation) and seek to know God more fully. Mystagogy is a lifelong pursuit.

Ministry   The response a baptized Christian makes to the call to serve Christ and his Church, according to their own abilities and talents. Many ministries require training and formation and the ministers are recognized publicly in a special commissioning rite. Some of these ministries include the ministry of lector, server, catechist, Eucharistic minister, and minister of the sick.

Getting in Touch

Spend a few moments reflecting on the following questions. You can use words or phrases as well as complete sentences in your responses. Remember, there are no right or wrong answers, just honest answers.

How did you feel about coming to the retreat today?

How did it feel to be welcomed to the retreat?

What did those who were involved in welcoming you do that made you feel welcome?

Why do you think you were welcomed in this way?

How do you feel right now about participating in the retreat?

Family Ties

Spend a few moments reflecting on the following questions. You can use words or phrases as well as complete sentences in your responses. Remember, there are no right or wrong answers, just honest answers. You will be asked to share your responses with your small group.

List three words you would use to describe your family.

1.

2.

3.

List some activities that bring your family together.

When is it most comforting or enjoyable to have a family member or members present in your life?

Share a time when being together as a family strengthened family ties.

Sacramental Litany

Leader: Through the waters of Baptism,

All: *We celebrate Christ's life in us.*

Leader: Through the sacred Bread and Wine of the Eucharist,

All: *We celebrate Christ's life in us.*

Leader: Through the Spirit who confirms our commitment to the Church,

All: *We celebrate Christ's life in us.*

Leader: Through the forgiveness of sins,

All: *We celebrate Christ's life in us.*

Leader: Through the healing of bodies and minds in anointing,

All: *We celebrate Christ's life in us.*

Leader: Through the witness of love in marriage,

All: *We celebrate Christ's life in us.*

Leader: Through the call to service in Holy Orders

All: *We celebrate Christ's life in us.*

Holy Spirit Imagery

Using words, phrases, symbols, and pictures, name who the Holy Spirit is for you at this time in your life. Include the images that came to you during the sound collage. Feel free to use images you heard others express as part of that exercise.

Gifts of the Holy Spirit

Wisdom is the ability to know with the heart; to be able to make complex things simple enough for a child to understand. Wisdom most accurately describes the way God knows everything. Only God is all-seeing, able to penetrate the innermost secrets of all creation. God shares that way of knowing with us through the Holy Spirit, who inspires humans to see things through the eyes of faith. The prophets and authors of Scripture are an example of this kind of knowing. For a beautiful and poetic description of wisdom, read the seventh chapter in the Book of Wisdom, verses 22–30.

Understanding is closely related to wisdom. It, too, is a way of seeing reality and knowing with the heart, but its focus is on seeing the relationship between things. Understanding helps us make sense of reality by helping us grasp how things are connected. When we understand something, we see what lies behind it, beneath it, around it. When we use the gift of understanding, we are able to make connections. Both wisdom and understanding are essential in helping us to make good decisions.

Knowledge is the gift that helps us distinguish between truth and falsehood, fact and fiction, the real and the imagined. This kind of awareness, though not as profound as wisdom, helps us sort through what we learn in our education and from experience in order that we may come to recognize what is true. Without the facts it is easy to get confused and make very poor judgments. All three gifts—wisdom, understanding, and knowledge—are necessary to help us see with the eyes of faith.

Courage or **fortitude** combines bravery and endurance. This gift helps us face danger, stand up for what we know is right, and act accordingly. For a Christian, courage comes from knowing we can trust God to be with us always. Courage is the backbone of moral strength. Knowing what to do in a given situation is not always enough to empower us to act morally. Courage demands an inner strength. Saint Paul put it this way in his second letter to Timothy, *". . . stir into flame the gift of God bestowed on you when my hands were laid upon you. The Spirit God has given us is no cowardly spirit, but rather one that makes us strong, loving, and wise"* (2 Timothy 1:6–7). There are many examples of courage at work in the Church. The most obvious are the martyrs, those men and women who were and are willing to endure suffering and even death in order to put their faith into practice.

Right judgment or **counsel** refers to the ability to look at a situation, discern what is the correct thing to do, and have the courage to do it. As you can see, the gift of right judgment relies on the gifts of wisdom, understanding, knowledge, and courage. This gift allows us to give ourselves and others good advice. We are able to do this if we pray, seek out the guidance of the Holy Spirit in Scripture and the teachings of the Church, and consult with others in the faith community.

Reverence or **piety** is a deep sense of love that leads us to deliberately seek out ways to please God. If we are reverent, we want to give honor and praise. This is the gift that helps us place God as the number-one priority in our lives. Reverence helps us make the prophet Micah's call "to live justly, love tenderly, and walk humbly with our God" a reality in our lives. The gift of reverence also encompasses everything that comes from God, so we are called as Christians to lovingly embrace all of God's creation, to love God by loving all that comes from God.

Wonder and awe in God's presence or **fear of the Lord** is the ability to perceive just how holy, powerful, wise, beautiful, and almighty God is. We experience this gift when we are caught speechless before the power of a storm, the vastness of the universe, or the beauty of a sunset. Sometimes being aware of just how awesome God really is, we are a bit overwhelmed. Scripture sometimes says people were terrified in God's presence, hence they named the gift fear of the Lord. Once such example is the story of the making of the covenant between God and the Israelites at Mount Sinai. Read the story in chapters 19 and 20 in the book of Exodus.

Prayer to the Holy Spirit

Come, Holy Spirit, fill the hearts of your faithful.

And kindle in them the fire of your love.

Send forth your Spirit and they shall be created.

And you will renew the face of the earth.

Lord, by the light of the Holy Spirit

you have taught the hearts of your faithful.

In the same Spirit help us choose what is right

and always rejoice in your consolation.

We ask this through Christ our Lord.

Amen

Session 1

Dear parent or guardian,

When you brought your child to be baptized you accepted the awesome responsibility of "training them in the practice of the faith" (*Rite of Baptism*, 39). In the course of the baptismal rite you were identified as the first and best teacher of your child and were entrusted with keeping the light of faith burning brightly in his or her life. Your presence at the first session for the Confirmation program spoke volumes about the faithfulness with which you have kept the promises you made so long ago.

As was discussed in the first session, this is not a class it is a journey. Your child has been called to take an important step on that journey which began years before at the baptismal font—the completion of his or her sacramental initiation as a full member of Christ's Church. Though your child is far more independent than in those early days, you remain his or her first and best teacher. Because of your unique relationship, if your child decides to enter into the Confirmation process, you will be called to journey with him or her as a guide along the way. He or she will need your continued support and encouragement. Your child will need your witness and example to understand what it means to live as a committed adult Catholic. He or she will need your prayers. As you help your child discern whether he or she is ready, willing, and able to prepare for the reception of the Sacrament of Confirmation, in addition to the questions on page 7 of your child's book ask yourself the following questions:

1. How have I responded to the call I received at my child's baptism to keep the light of faith burning brightly in his or her life? How has responding to that call changed me, challenged me, blessed me?

2. What have I learned as a result of my own faith journey that I can pass on to my child for consideration on the next step of the journey?

3. Can our family realistically undertake the preparation process at this time? Do we have the energy and time such a commitment requires, or should we wait?

Thank you for all that you have done to keep the light of faith burning brightly. Thank you for making the time to consider and honestly assess whether the time is right for helping your child complete his or her sacramental initiation as a Catholic. Know we will be praying for you and your child as you make this important decision. Please contact a member of the catechetical staff if you have any questions or would like to discuss any of the issues raised during the first session. Once you make your decision, you are expected to notify the person mentioned by the date given during the first session.

Session 2

Dear parent or guardian,

The focus of Session 2 was the reality of sin in both its personal and social dimensions. Also discussed was the gospel's call to repent and reform our own lives and the social structures and institutions corrupted by sin. The following points were made:

- The reality of the presence of sin cannot be denied or dismissed casually. All of us are affected by the reality of sin. No one escapes the consequences of sin, which the Church identifies as the experiences of evil, suffering, and death.

- The most common effect of sin that the majority of us experience is its impact on relationships. To demonstrate this point the candidates and mentors turned to the book of Genesis to reflect on the story of the temptation and fall of the first humans.

- Sin affects society. Sin is never an isolated act—our actions always affect others.

- Sin needs to be actively challenged. In following Jesus, Christians must reject the ways of evil and repair the damage caused by sin.

- The Church, through the power of the Holy Spirit, continues Jesus' work of healing and salvation through the Sacrament of Reconciliation.

Before the next session candidates are to read the story of Saint Augustine of Hippo and answer the reflection questions on page 16, and study the Scripture verses and the Language of Faith on page 17 in the candidate's book. They are encouraged to celebrate the Sacrament of Reconciliation. Candidates recorded in their books the times and days when Reconciliation is celebrated in their parish. Plan a time when you and your child can celebrate this sacrament together.

Your child was also asked to begin thinking about how he or she might use his or her gifts and talents to work for peace and justice and actively repair the damage caused by sin. As your child enters this process take some time to reflect on the gifts and talents you see in him or her. Find a way to share what you see. A short note of affirmation listing your child's gifts might be one option. Modeling the response a mature Christian makes to sin, share with your child how you acknowledge sin and ask God and others for forgiveness.

Session 3

Dear parent or guardian,

The focus of Session 3 was God's revelation in Scripture. The following points were made:

- It is more accurate to think of the Bible as a library of books rather than a single volume. The Catholic Canon of Sacred Scripture contains two testaments—the Old Testament, comprised of 46 books and the New Testament, which contains 27 books. The Gospels, found in the New Testament, are the primary source for learning about the life and teachings of Jesus Christ, who is the living Word of God.

- The truth contained in Scripture cannot be fully understood by looking at individual passages or individual books. Therefore, each book should be seen in relation to all the other books. The whole truth can be known only through studying the whole book.

- God is the author of Scripture. He chose certain people and, through the power of the Holy Spirit, used their talents as writers, prophets, and teachers to reveal himself. The Holy Spirit continues to work today to open our minds and hearts to the word of God so that we may understand more clearly what God is trying to tell us.

- Catholics interpret the Bible in a contextual, or spiritual sense. This means that one looks into the meaning or deeper truths behind the actual words. The intent of the authors, the audience to whom the authors were writing, and the historical and cultural events and understandings that framed the writing of a particular book are important factors to consider when interpreting a given passage or book.

Before the next session candidates are to complete the exercise found on page 22, read the story of St. Mark and answer the reflection questions on page 24, and study the Scripture verses and the Language of Faith on page 25 in the candidate's book.

This Bible is more than a book—even a holy book. It is the living word of God. Recall a favorite Scripture passage of yours. Find some time before the next session to sit with your child and read the passage together. Share with your child why this passage is significant to you. Share with your child some of what you have learned from the Scriptures about God, about yourself, about life. Purchase a holy card or prayer card with a Scripture quote on it and give it to your child. Many religious goods stores carry these items.

Session 4

Dear parent or guardian,

The focus of Session 4 was the Holy Spirit in our lives. The following points were made:

- Faith is assent to and trust in the truth. God proves to us by both word and action that he can be trusted.

- Faith is a personal act—the free response of the human person to God's invitation to trust. Faith is the gift of an ongoing relationship between an individual and the divine (*Catechism of the Catholic Church*, 52, 142). We trust in God's ultimate goodness and love for us.

- Faith is a communal act. As Christians who profess a belief in the Triune God, we are called to be in a relationship not only with God, but with each other and with all of creation.

- Faith allows us to see, feel, and forge new connectedness. As one's faith continues to deepen, one can begin to understand and see things from new perspectives. Bonding and connectedness are some of what is celebrated in the Sacrament of Confirmation.

Before the next session candidates are to complete the exercise found on page 27, read the story of Saint Thérèse of Lisieux and answer the reflection questions on page 32, and study the Scripture verses and the Language of Faith on page 33 in the candidate's book.

Before the next session there will be a special liturgy incorporating the renewal of baptismal promises. The candidates' families are asked to be present with them for this celebration. The liturgy will take place on _____

date

_____ at _____.

time   location

Along with the candidates and mentors, parents are also asked to participate in the next session.

Session 5

Dear parent or guardian,

Thank you for celebrating the renewal of baptismal promises with the Confirmation candidates and participating in the session that followed. Your support of the Confirmation candidate is an inspiration to him or her. Your willingness to participate in this journey has been an important part of your child's preparation. You are your child's first and best teacher, a living example of what it means to be a committed adult Catholic.

After reflecting on their baptismal vows, candidates were asked to consider the many ways, that through the gifts of the Holy Spirit, the work and ministry of Jesus are continued in our Church and community for the common good. Common good assumes a respect and dignity for the human person and for those things needed for a truly human life: food, clothing, health, and education.

At the fifth session your child was given a **Service Commitment** form. He or she is asked to complete and return it at the next session. As part of this exercise recall a time when you extended yourself in service to another. Share with your child what that experience meant to you and what you learned from the experience. Help your child honestly assess his or her own talents and gifts. Ask your child if he or she would like you to participate in the community service project with him or her. Make sure your child understands that you are willing to be involved, but respect his or her wishes if he or she chooses to do service on his or her own. You might offer to do a different type of community service as a way of standing in solidarity with your child.

Before the next session each candidate is to fill out the **Service Commitment** form and his or her copy of the service commitment form on page 39, read the story of Saint Elizabeth and answer the reflection questions on page 40, and study the Scripture verses and the Language of Faith on page 41 in the candidate's book.

Session 6

Dear parent or guardian,

Our focus in Session 6 was on Apostolic and ecclesial Tradition with an emphasis on the laying on of hands. The following points were made:

- Tradition and Scripture are bound closely together and thus both must be accepted and honored with equal sentiments of devotion and reverence (CCC, 82). The living Tradition of the Church is seen as necessary in accurately interpreting the sacred texts.

- The Church differentiates between Apostolic Traditions and ecclesial traditions. Scriptures and Apostolic Traditions contain the "sacred deposit" of faith. Church doctrines guide us in our understanding of God and his plan for us. These Traditions cannot be fundamentally changed, for they have been divinely ordained and the entire people of God are asked to adhere faithfully to the these teachings (CCC, 84).

- Ecclesial traditions refer to customs and practices that developed in local churches for particular reasons in a given time and place. These traditions can be maintained, changed, or even dropped under the guidance of the Holy Spirit through the pope and other bishops (CCC, 83).

- One element that incorporates both Apostolic and ecclesial traditions is in the area of prayer. The traditions of our Church provide for private or individual prayer, shared prayer, and liturgical prayer. Saying the Rosary, and reading Scripture together with a group of people would be an example of shared prayer. Mass and the celebration of the sacraments would be an example of liturgical prayer.

- All prayer takes five basic forms—praise, petition, thanksgiving, intercession, and contrition or sorrow. We are encouraged to pray often, using whatever forms and aids are helpful.

- The laying on of hands is an ancient symbol. In the early Church the apostles imparted the gift of the Spirit by laying hands on the newly baptized. This ritual gesture is seen in the Catholic tradition as the origin of the Sacrament of Confirmation. In the celebration of Confirmation, the bishop and the priests present for the celebration will lay, or impose, hands on the candidates while the bishop prays for the coming of the Spirit.

Before the next session candidates are to complete the activity on page 47, read about Saint Hildegard of Bingen and answer the reflection questions on page 48, and study the Scripture verses and the Language of Faith on page 49 in the candidate's book.

Find some time to reflect on some of the traditions of the Church, especially traditions of prayer and worship that are meaningful to you. Choose one of those traditions to help you pray for your child. For instance, you might say a rosary or attend daily Mass and receive Communion asking God to bless your child in a special way. After you decide what tradition you will choose, find a way to let your child know that you are praying for them in this way.

Session 7

Dear parent or guardian,

Our focus in Session 7 was the use of symbols and rituals with an emphasis on anointing. The following points were made:

- As a sacramental church we believe that God speaks to us through symbols and rituals. That is why color, scent, liturgical artifacts, touch, music, the spoken word, and silence are so much a part of our prayer life as Catholics.

- There are many symbols used in our faith tradition. In this session candidates and mentors explored the symbolic meaning of the Paschal candle, incense, color, and sacred oils, all of which play a key role in the celebration of Confirmation.

- Rituals and symbolic gestures are also significant in Catholic worship. In this session the candidates and mentors focused on the ritual of anointing. This ritual was believed to confer strength, wisdom, and courage and was used to designate God's chosen servants. The anointing with oil in the Rite of Confirmation symbolizes selection and strength, as it did in biblical times (CCC, 1293). It also has become synonymous with the Holy Spirit (CCC, 695). During the Sacrament of Confirmation the bishop or presider says, *"N., be sealed with the Gift of the Holy Spirit,"* as he makes a sign of the cross on the forehead of each candidate. "By this anointing the confirmand receives the 'mark,' the seal of the Holy Spirit. Being marked with the sign of the cross is a reminder that we share in the life of Christ" (CCC, 265). The "Amen" response by the candidates is their personal affirmation of their desire to witness to Christ in the world (CCC, 1064).

Before the retreat each candidate is to complete the crossword puzzle found on page 55. Before the next session each candidate is to read the story about the woman who anointed Jesus and answer the reflection questions on page 56 and study the Scripture verses and the Language of Faith on page 57 in the candidate's book.

As part of the preparation process each candidate is asked to make a retreat. Your child was given a letter regarding details about the retreat and a permission slip and medical release form which should be completed and returned to the retreat director the day of the retreat.

We are nearing the end of the preparation period. Please make time to talk with your child about how he or she feels about celebrating the Sacrament of Confirmation. Your child may still feel unready to make a public confession of faith or unable to take on the demands of a fully initiated member of the Church—regular attendance at Sunday Mass, frequent reception of the sacraments, a disciplined prayer life, a commitment to ministry and ongoing service to the community. Reassure your child of your continuing support.

It is also time to make sure all the details of the preparation process have been attended to. Has your child completed the service project? Has your child chosen a Confirmation name and a sponsor? Have you communicated that information to the parish? If you have any questions or concerns about these or other issues please contact a member of the catechetical staff.

Remember that there is an eighth session on mystagogy that is required for all those who are confirmed.

Session 8

Dear parent or guardian,

In Session 8 the newly confirmed acknowledged an important milestone. At this time they are again being named and called. They are named disciples and called to active ministry. The following points were made:

- Sacramental initiation plunges us into a lifelong relationship with God and his people. Though the rituals of initiation are limited in time and space, they lead us into the much richer and deeper reality of Trinitarian life. As baptized and confirmed Catholics we are called to live no longer for ourselves but in Christ. The newly confirmed will continue to need your prayers and guidance in order to better understand the mysteries of faith and the awesomeness of our God. The work of mystagogy is always ongoing.

- Ministry is the right and responsibility of all the baptized. Strengthened by the gifts of the Holy Spirit, the newly confirmed need to be reminded of their baptismal call and invited to participate more fully in the mission and ministry of the Church.

Candidates and mentors were asked to identify the highlights of the journey. The result of this reflection will be displayed in the parish in the form of a mosaic. As a parent reflect on what has been significant for you in this process. Spend some time in prayer giving thanks for these gifts.

Looking toward the future candidates were asked to complete the **Spiritual Health Inventory** found on page 63. You may find this a valuable exercise to do with your child, modeling for them the need for ongoing reflection and re-commitment to ministry. Read the story of Charles Lwanga and the African martyrs with your child. Tell your child about someone who has been a model or witness for you. Encourage your child to follow up on any interest shown in parish ministries. Finally, tell your child how proud you are of his or her willingness to grow in faith.

Thank you for all that you have done and been for your child and for our parish faith community. Thank you for your witness to us. May you and your child continue to grow in wisdom and grace and find in our community support for continuing to be faithful disciples of Christ.

The Sacrament of Reconciliation

Examination of Conscience

1. Look at your life in the light of the Beatitudes, the Ten Commandments, the Great Commandment, and the precepts of the Church.

2. Ask yourself:
   - Where have I fallen short of what God wants for me?
   - Whom have I hurt?
   - What have I done that I knew was wrong?
   - What have I not done that I should have done?
   - Are there serious sins I neglected to mention the last time I confessed?
   - Have I done penance and tried as hard as I could to make up for past sins?
   - Have I made the necessary changes in bad habits?
   - What areas am I still having trouble with?
   - Am I sincerely sorry for all my sins?

3. In addition to any sins you are confessing, you may wish to talk about one or more of the above questions with the priest.

4. Pray for the Holy Spirit's help in making a fresh start.

The Individual Rite of Reconciliation

1. **Welcome**

   The priest will welcome you and invite you to pray the Sign of the Cross.

2. **Reading from Scripture**

   The priest may read or recite a passage from the Bible. You may be invited by the priest to read the Scripture yourself.

3. **Confession of Sins and Giving of Penance**

   Tell your sins to the priest. The priest will talk with you about how to do better. Then the priest will give you a penance.

4. **Act of Contrition**

   Pray an Act of Contrition.

5. **Absolution**

   The priest will hold his hand over your head and pray the prayer of absolution. As he prays the final words, he will make the Sign of the Cross.

6. **Closing Prayer**

   The priest will pray, "Give thanks to the Lord, for he is good." You answer, "His mercy endures forever." Then the priest will dismiss you.

   After celebrating the sacrament, carry out your penance as soon as possible.

The Communal Rite of Reconciliation

Before celebrating the Sacrament of Reconciliation, take time to examine your conscience. Pray for the Holy Spirit's help.

1. Introductory Rites

Join in singing the opening hymn. The priest will greet the assembly and lead you in the opening prayer.

2. Reading from Scripture

Listen to the word of God. There may be more than one reading, with a hymn or psalm in between. The last reading will be from one of the Gospels.

3. Homily

Listen as the priest helps you understand the meaning of the Scriptures.

4. Examination of Conscience with Litany of Contrition and the Lords' prayer

After the homily there will be a time of silence. The priest may lead the assembly in an examination of conscience. This is followed by the prayer of confession and the litany or song. Then all will pray the Lord's Prayer together.

5. Individual Confession, Giving of Penance, and Absolution

While you wait your turn to talk with the priest, you may pray quietly or join in singing. When it is your turn, confess your sins to the priest. He will talk to you about how to do better and give you a penance. Then the priest will pray the prayer of absolution.

6. Closing Rite

After everyone has confessed individually, join in singing or praying a song or litany of Thanksgiving. The priest will lead the closing prayer and bless the assembly. Then the priest or deacon will dismiss the assembly.

After celebrating the sacrament, carry out your penance as soon as possible.

Catholic Prayers

Glory to the Father (Doxology)

Glory to the Father,

and to the Son,

and to the Holy Spirit.

As it was in the beginning, is now,

and will be forever. Amen.

Act of Faith

O God, we firmly believe that you are one God in three divine Persons, Father, Son and Holy Spirit; we believe that your divine Son became man and died for our sins, and that he will come to judge the living and the dead. We believe these and all the truths that the holy Catholic Church teaches, because you have revealed them, and you can neither deceive nor be deceived.

Act of Hope

O God, relying on your almighty power and your endless mercy and promises, we hope to gain pardon for our sins, the help of your grace, and life everlasting, through the saving actions of Jesus Christ, our Lord and Redeemer.

Act of Love

O God, we love you above all things, with our whole heart and soul, because you are all-good and worthy of all love. We love our neighbor as ourselves for the love of you. We forgive all who have injured us and ask pardon of all whom we have injured.

Act of Contrition

My God, I am sorry for my sins with all my heart. In choosing to do wrong and failing to do good, I have sinned against you whom I should love above all things. I firmly intend, with your help, to do penance, to sin no more, and to avoid whatever leads me to sin. Our Savior Jesus Christ suffered and died for us. In his name, my God, have mercy.

The Jesus Prayer

Lord Jesus Christ, Son of God, have mercy on me, a sinner. Amen.